mind & hand
CONTEMPORARY STUDIO FURNITURE

The Furniture Society

Technical content by Jean Aslund | Photography by Douglas Congdon-Martin

Schiffer Publishing Ltd®
4880 Lower Valley Road, Atglen, Pennsylvania 19310

Other Schiffer Books on Related Subjects:
Esherick, Maloof, and Nakashima: Homes of the Master Wood Artisans
    ISBN: 978-0-7643-3202-9 $49.99
Studio Furniture: from Today's Leading Woodworkers.
    ISBN: 978-0-7643-3287-6 $39.99
Wood Art Todat 2. ISBN: 978097643-4 $50.00y

Designed by Justin Watkinson
Cover by Bruce Waters
Type set in ChaletComprime/PreciousSerif/Century Gothic

ISBN: 978-0-7643-4115-1
Printed in China

Schiffer Books are available at special discounts for bulk purchases for sales promotions or premiums. Special editions, including personalized covers, corporate imprints, and excerpts can be created in large quantities for special needs. For more information contact the publisher:

Published by Schiffer Publishing Ltd.
4880 Lower Valley Road
Atglen, PA 19310
Phone: (610) 593-1777; Fax: (610) 593-2002
E-mail: Info@schifferbooks.com

For the largest selection of fine reference books on this and related subjects,
please visit our website at **www.schifferbooks.com**
We are always looking for people to write books on new and related subjects.
If you have an idea for a book, please contact us at
proposals@schifferbooks.com

This book may be purchased from the publisher.
Include $5.00 for shipping.
Please try your bookstore first.
You may write for a free catalog.

In Europe, Schiffer books are distributed by
Bushwood Books
6 Marksbury Ave.
Kew Gardens
Surrey TW9 4JF England
Phone: 44 (0) 20 8392 8585; Fax: 44 (0) 20 8392 9876
E-mail: info@bushwoodbooks.co.uk
Website: www.bushwoodbooks.co.uk

contents

foreword

Alf Sharp

When I think of Furniture Society conferences, a thriving rural European village festival often comes to mind. They are indeed festive events, where good friends, who are more than not, separated by many miles and many months, get together to talk about the things they love the most, and also to have a lot of fun. But then, I realize there's so much more to the image I am portraying - intelligent discourse, visual motivation, creative ferment. What it is, is a community, one that gathers in-person only once a year, but that exists in the hearts of its members throughout the rest of the year.

After the first conference that I attended, in Smithville, Tenn. in 1999, I felt as if my creative batteries had been recharged for a year, and I decided to never miss another conference, if at all possible. I've been able to keep that resolution, and have considered every event to be as much an investment in my career as any tool purchase or workshop I might have made.

This publication is a visual portrayal showing the variety and excitement of a Furniture Society annual conference, in this case Cambridge, Mass. in 2010.

There are always numerous exhibits, some sponsored by the Society, others by interested parties such as galleries and museums. The Members' Gallery is always a completely unpredictable but delightful assemblage of whatever the participants bring, and provides a real-world vitality that comes from displaying work across the entire spectrum of design sophistication and technical proficiency.

Visually, the Cambridge conference was particularly juicy, for several reasons. The featured theme exhibition was "Outdoor Furniture", which really propelled the creative processes for our members, and the finished works, displayed all over the commons in front of the Kresge Auditorium were a huge hit. All the pieces on display were available for anyone to use or explore however they chose, and this display became a very popular attraction for the entire MIT community including a wedding party who took the opportunity to pose for photographs on and in front of the giant straw sitting-room furniture! The expansive space available inside the Kresge Auditorium allowed for a very large member's gallery, and the creative presentation of these works was a testament to the engineering genius of our MIT participants. The juried exhibit, "Six Degrees of Separation" drew entries from makers spread across the New England states, traditionally one of the strongest hot-beds of studio furniture-making. In addition to these attractions, the Society's auction committee had assembled one of the most impressive collections of important work by our members ever offered. All these items were on display throughout the week as well. Finally, the numerous artists' presentations that are always an integral part of conference offered hours of enjoyment from the best contemporary furniture work being done in the world.

This publication is dedicated to presenting the visual experience of the 2010 MIT Furniture Society conference. A book such as this can only begin to hint at the vibrant culture of creativity and innovation, not to mention the party atmosphere that is a Furniture Society conference. Anyone interested in the field of small-shop custom furniture-making, whether as maker or consumer, should make plans to attend every conference the Society organizes.

Alf Sharp
President, Board of Trustees
The Furniture Society

preface

This book demonstrates the beautiful contemporary furniture that is designed and made by furniture makers who are members of The Furniture Society. The society's conference, *Fusions: Minds & Hands Shaping Our Future*, convened June 16-19, 2010, at the Massachusetts Institute of Technology (MIT), Cambridge. The cultural richness of Boston, with its many galleries, museums, and educational institutions, greatly enhanced the conference proceedings. In focusing on the theme of fusion—the merging of diverse, distinct elements into a unified whole—the conference brought together makers and designers, collectors, educators, and curators to address the role of furniture in today's society as well as the historical context and future of contemporary furniture.

The Furniture Society is a nonprofit, educational organization founded in 1996. Its mission is to advance the art of furniture making by inspiring creativity, promoting excellence, and fostering an understanding of this art and its place in society.

Built on a tradition of volunteerism, The Furniture Society works to realize its mission through educational programs, publications, exhibitions, recognition of excellence in the field, and annual conferences. With members from across the United States and Canada, as well as numerous other countries around the world, the Furniture Society represents a broad cross-section of furniture makers, museum and gallery professionals, scholars, journalists, and others involved with the field of furniture in many different ways.

The Society sponsors a variety of programs that contribute to the education and enrichment of members and the public. This book reflects its programs to showcase and inspire fine woodworking. Derived from its members, the beautiful, hand-crafted furniture displayed here represents contemporary efforts to design and build relevant styles that can be useful for today's customers. These pieces represent the fluid relationships between the creator's mind and hands, tools and materials, maker and client. They combine the latest techniques and theories while focusing on distinct elements that bring together the makers and designers, collectors, educators, and curators to address the role of furniture in today's society. The historical content of American furniture is acknowledged as well as the future of contemporary furniture.

The 2010 Furniture Society Award of Distinction was presented to John Cederquist, furniture maker and sculptor, who lives in Capistrano Beach, California. "John has a voice like no other furniture maker today," said Miguel Gomez-Ibanez, chair of the 2010 Award of Distinction Committee, in announcing the award. "His furniture includes references to contemporary culture, to comic strips, and traditional Japanese block prints. As a measure of his talent, he has inspired a generation of furniture makers to think of their art in new ways without spawning a group of imitators."

In a 2006 review of Cederquist's show, "Kosode Built as in a Dream," in *The New York Times,* the writer, Grace Clueck, described these kimonos, in the shape of garments on display, as "Ingeniously wrought of various kinds of wood, put together and painted so as to simulate the folds and draperies of actual garments. Their surfaces are then adorned with extravagant motifs that sometimes refer to masterpieces of an earlier age... these robes actually open to reveal interior systems of shelves and drawers."

Cederquist has received two National Endowment for the Arts Fellowships, in 1975 and 1986. In 2002 he was elected to the American Craft Council College of Fellows. Leading museums hold his work in their collections, among them the Philadelphia Museum of Art, the Mint Museum of Craft + Design, the Museum of the Art Institute of Chicago, Yale University Art Gallery, and the M.H. de Young Memorial Museum–Fine Arts Museums of San Francisco.

INTRODUCTION
shaping the future

Richard Oedel

This book displays the fluid relationships between mind and hand, tool and material, maker and client, technique and theory. In seeking to merge diverse, distinct elements into their designs, the makers address the roles of furniture in today's society as well as acknowledging its historical context and pointing to the future of contemporary studio furniture.

In 2007, Miguel Gomez-Ibanez and I discussed having a Furniture Society Conference in New England. Yes, we both thought it was important to have it in Boston, and that it be inclusive, with the Rhode Island School of Design, Boston University (the original home of the Program in Artisanry – the legendary program set up and run by Jere Osgood and Alphonse Mattia), UMass South Dartmouth (the current home of the PIA), as well as the North Bennet Street School, Mass College of Art, and anyone else who had a furniture design program as part of the conference. But we didn't know if anyone else shared that idea, so I started calling on furniture makers in the area.

The response was overwhelmingly positive and the people with whom I had talked enthusiastically endorsed the plan (if it could indeed be called a plan) to bring the conference to Boston.

In May, I called around to contacts in Boston. Did Boston University want to host the conference? No, they had no furniture program and they had no interest in the history of the PIA program. How about RISD? No, maybe in future years, but they could not spare the time to organize and host. Harvard? Yoav Liberman was very helpful, but in the end, there was little interest. That brought me to June, 2007, and the Furniture Conference in Victoria, British Columbia.

Standing in a line, waiting for registration, I noticed Hayami Arakawa who had been at Madison in the furniture program and had helped Wendy Maruyama with the San Diego conference; we had been in touch about a possible shop space for him when he moved to Boston and started working at MIT in Cambridge. Standing next to him was a person I did not recognize, but whose name tag indicated he was from MIT and probably knew Hayami. I just sidled up to Ken Stone and asked him if he had any interest in hosting the conference at MIT. Nothing ventured, nothing gained. He looked at me as though I had two heads, mumbled something non-committal, and I headed off to experience the Victoria 2007 Furniture Society Conference. A month later, Ken e-mailed me and we had lunch to talk about the conference. Yes, there was interest. Yes, it might work with MIT being host. Yes, he was personally interested. And yes, he was a good furniture maker with deep connections throughout the MIT community.

But better still was the connection between MIT and furniture, as well as a firm university commitment to the arts. The Greene brothers were both MIT graduates, and Greene and Greene furniture was undergoing a resurgence with an exhibit at the Boston Museum of Fine Arts. George Nakashima was an MIT grad and his place as a progenitor of American Contemporary Furniture was firmly established. The best connection, however, was MIT itself. Founded in 1861 with an emphasis on applied technology at the undergraduate and graduate levels, the first and only motto of MIT is *"Mens et Manus,"* or "Mind and Hand," a reference to the desire that all MIT graduates should not only work with their minds but also have a hands-on relationship with their field and with the world at large.

A decade before the names Ruskin and Morris would be known for their Arts and Crafts philosophies, MIT was explicitly engaging the minds and hands of their students in their studies. Continuing until the present day, MIT has a vast array of outside activities to challenge their students, including the largest number of varsity teams at any American university. And Ken Stone has control of the shop where these engineers and scientists put their ideas into wood, steel and plastic.

Ken immediately received a positive response from his dean and started using his considerable political capital within the MIT community to build a support base for the conference and for furniture design and making at the university.

When Ken invited me to present the plans and project at MIT, the reception we received could only be considered warm and welcoming, continuing with every interaction throughout the conference. Mike Foley and his staff, who kept us on-time and focused; Cathi Levine, who organized the housing, and Alex Slocum, who agreed to speak, welcoming The Furniture Society to MIT, were just some of the people who made the conference a success. They added their expertise to ours in ways we could not have imagined, all while removing obstacles from our path. And it was exciting to be at MIT. Where else could you borrow a forklift from Plasma Physics to unload a 12-foot-tall chair and place it in front of Eero Saarinen's iconic chapel? From the earliest days to the final cleanup, MIT was the perfect host, allowing the Boston Committee to focus on the exhibits and programming. This volume is meant to be a sampling of the exhibits and the work that goes on in our minds as our hands create the pieces you see here.

—Richard Oedel, Ken Stone and the Boston Committee: Miguel Gomez-Ibanez, Mark DelGiudice, Beth Ann Gerstein, Hayami Arakawa, Mitch Ryerson, Frank Burns, Earl Powell, Leah Woods and Shaun Bullens

We hope that you enjoy the work as well as the vignettes from the conference. We certainly did.

Bill Garbus

The Furniture Society members have contributed their work to this study of contemporary designs. The Members' Gallery is a tradition that traces back to the first Furniture Society conference in 1998. Acceptance of work is non-competitive. There is no jury or committee judging the work. As long as the piece fits within the size criteria, the work is accepted. This offers a chance for any Furniture Society member to display her or his work to a wide audience of colleagues, collectors, and the general public for a few days during the annual conference. Many Society members have limited or no other opportunities to show their work, especially since there are very few galleries remaining that show studio furniture, so this is a good opportunity for the participants to get feedback on their work.

In most conferences the members' gallery is housed in a space that was intended for the display of fine art. But this gallery was housed in the very dramatic lobby of MIT's Kresge Auditorium, an important architectural landmark designed by Aero Saarinen. It was a challenge to plan the gallery in this magnificent unique space, that was not designed for a gallery function. The entire curving front wall is glass, which made it difficult to view the work when the direct sun came streaming in. The limited number of walls were curved and made of concrete, so customized hangers were required to support all wall-mounted cabinets. These were well designed and fabricated from aircraft cable and aluminum by Ken Stone, the MIT fabrication lab director. Adding to the already tight space challenge was the temporary photo studio for this publication that was inserted at the last minute!

Planning, coordinating, and communicating took months and was especially intense in the last few weeks prior to the conference. Installing the work in the gallery is always a scramble, because the members deliver their work as they arrive at the conference and the show must be installed in one very hectic day.

The Members' Gallery was organized and managed by volunteers. Glen Guarino, with assistance from his wife, Marie, and Bill Garbus were co-managers for the Gallery.

Garry Knox Bennett
Summer Kindling
Steam-bent oak & maple
9.5"x27"x13"

Bruce P. Bradford
Winston Salem, NC

Bruce P. Bradford
Floating Hall Table
Maple, birch, cherry
27.5"x45"x14.25"

Robert Bragg
Cantilever Rocking Chair
Walnut, maple
40"x25"x40"

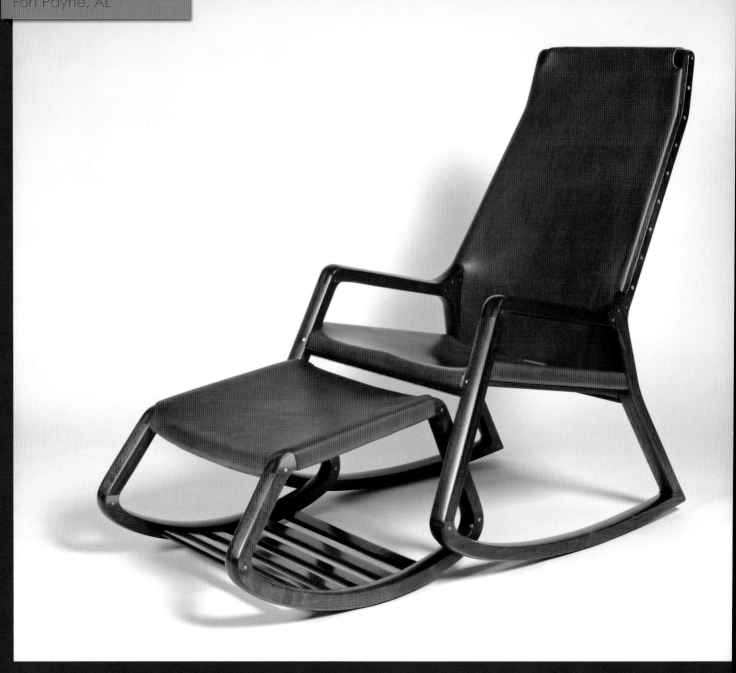

Keith Cochran
Rocking Stool
American black walnut, natural tan leather,
brass pins, rubbed tung oil, wax
15"x21.5"x24"

Randy, Keith
& Dylan Cochran
Lookout Mountain Rocker
American black walnut or sassafrass,
natural tan leather, brass pins, rubbed tung oil, wax
26"x34"x42"

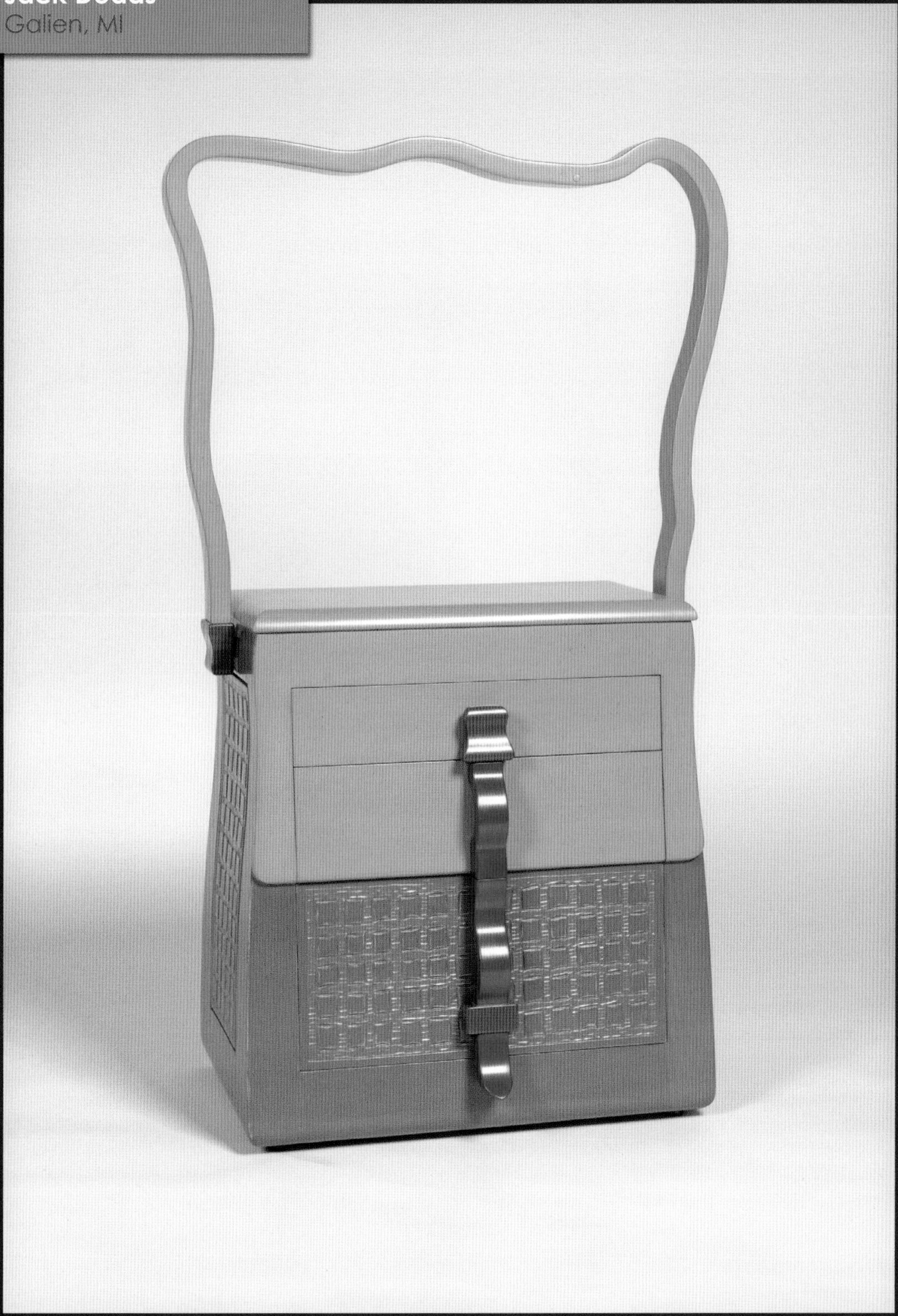

Jack Dodds
*Darlene's Got
A Brand New Bag*
Tulip poplar, hard maple,
cherry, milk paint,
wipe-on poly
25"x24"x16"

Karen Ernst
Notch Mirror & Shelf
Basswood & milk paint
30"x14"

Tor Faegre
Ash Arm Chair
Bent ash, plywood

Amy Forsyth
Bechtelsville, PA

Amy Forsyth
Jere's Table
Walnut, bloodwood,
milk-painted mahogany

Gail Fredell
Asheville, NC

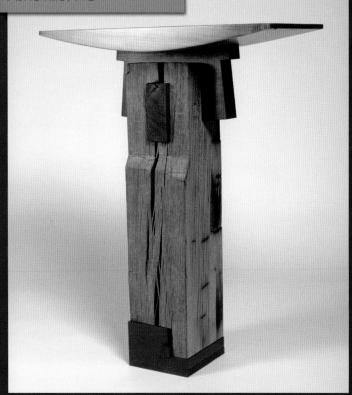

Gail Fredell
1006 Creston Road
Oak, steel, cherry
10"x29"x35"

Bill Garbus
Leaf Table
Honduran mahogany, India ink, Alkyd artists's paint, lacquer
21"x32"x17"

Brian Gladwell & Jason Schneider
Regina, SK, Canada & Snowmass Village, CO

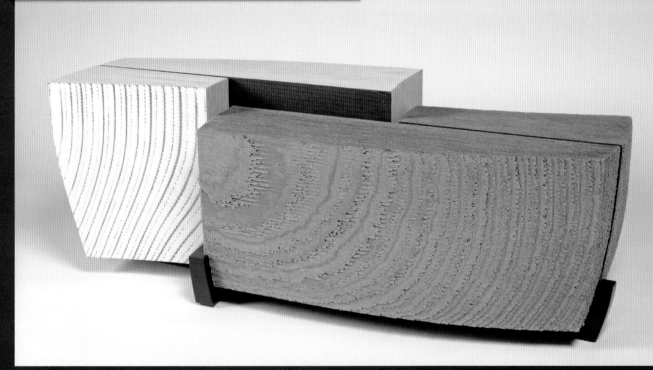

**Brian Gladwell
& Jason Schneider**
Untitled
Cardboard, wood,
wallboard compound
16"x20"x45"

Andrew Glantz
Scottsdale, AZ

Andrew Glantz
Entrance Table
Black walnut, curly maple
48"x15"x34"

Andrew Glenn & Lance Patterson
Boston, MA

Jenna Goldberg
Providence, RI

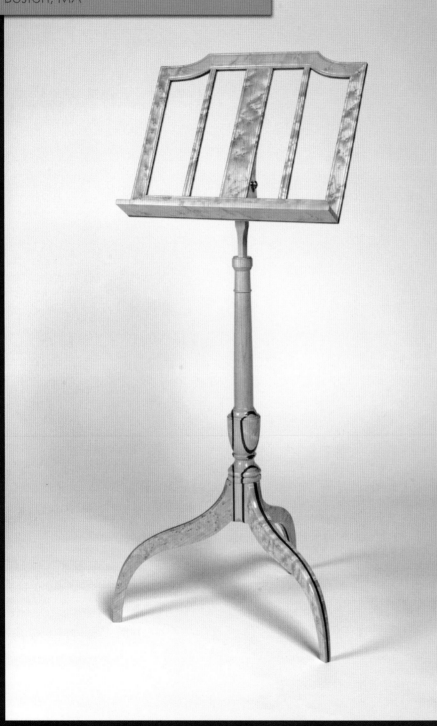

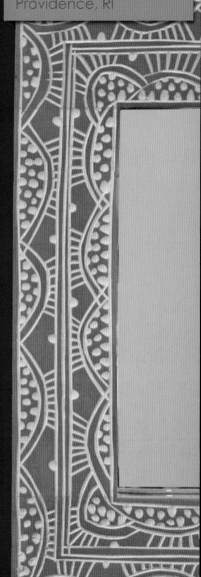

Andrew Glenn, maker
Lance Patterson, design
Music Stand

Jenna Goldberg
Orange Mirror
Painted & carved basswood
16"x2"x26"

Glen G. Guarino
Arabesque
Mozambique shedua & ebonized sapele
29.75"x37.5"x18"

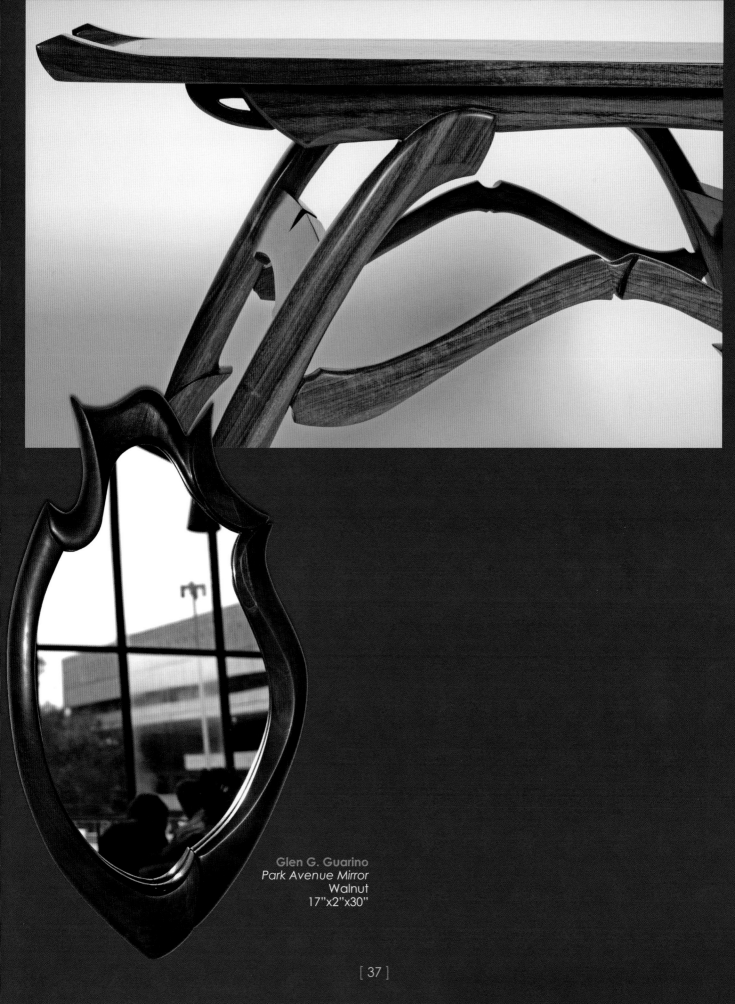

Glen G. Guarino
Park Avenue Mirror
Walnut
17"x2"x30"

Peter Handler
Philadelphia, PA

Peter Handler
Maldives Table
Coconut palm plywood, gold leaf, anodized aluminum
15"x23"x48"

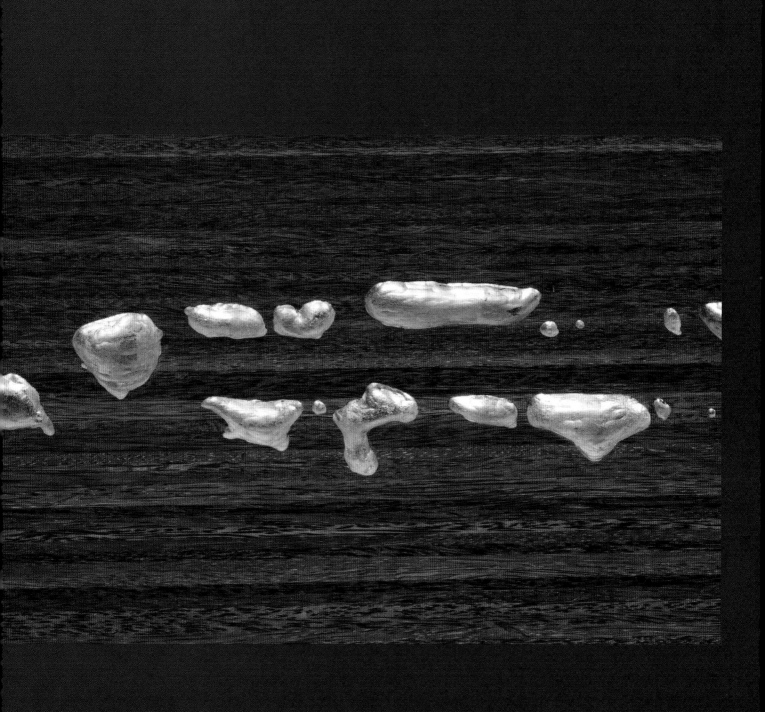

Katie Hudnall
Magpie Cabinet
6"x6"x24"

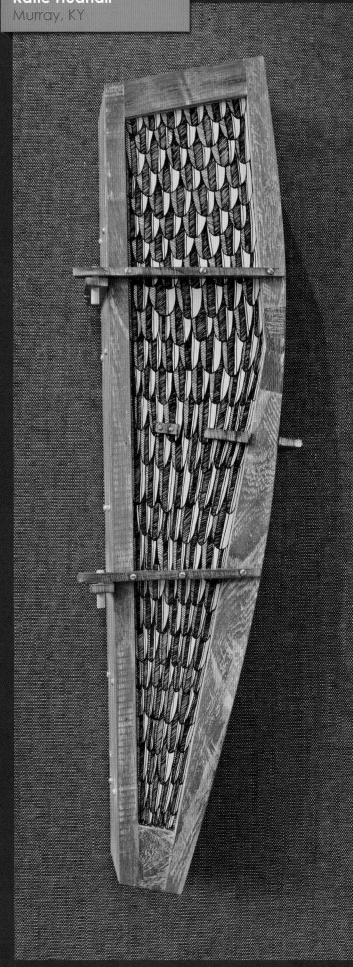

Katie Hudnall
Magpie Cabinet
6"x6"x24"

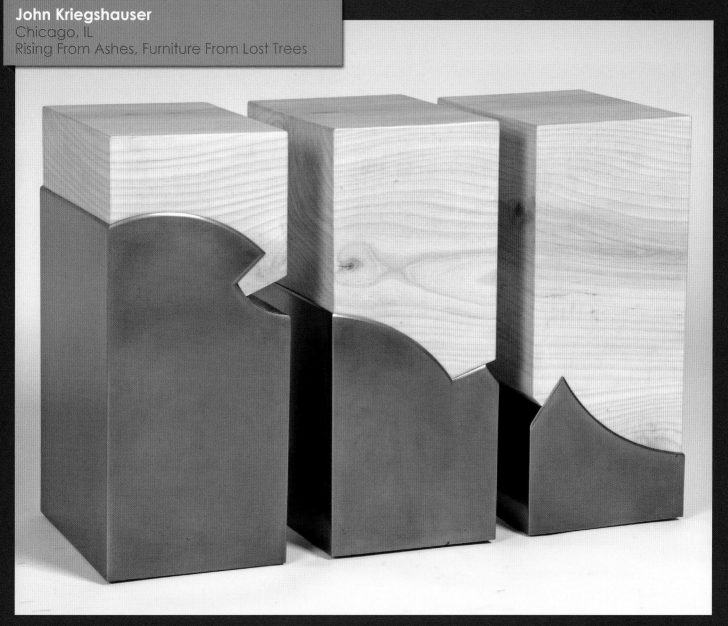

John Kriegshauser
Chicago, IL
Rising From Ashes, Furniture From Lost Trees

John Kriegshauser
Tansu Chest
Ash and cast aluminum

Justin Kramer
San Diego, CA

Justin Kramer
Untitled chair
Walnut, zebrawood

Michael Landberg
Wolfeboro, NH

Michael Landberg
Skewed Perception
Poplar, Peruvian walnut, red oak,
satin hand-rubbed finish
24"x24"x12"

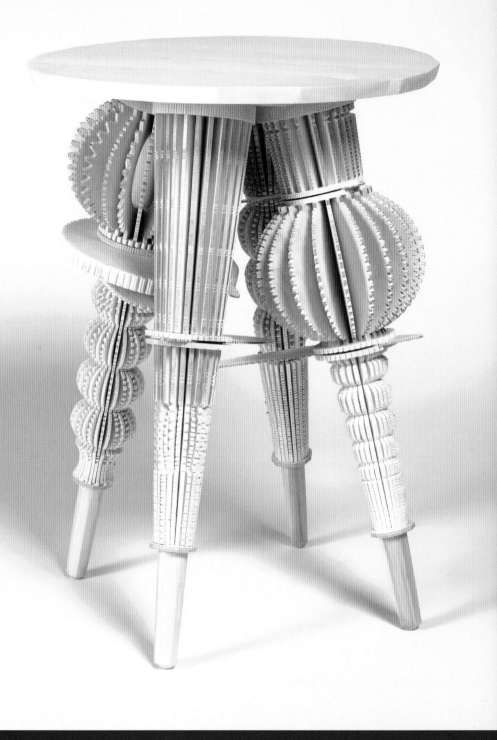

Po Shun Leong
Prototype Side Table
Bleached maple
8" diameter x 24"

Derrick Method
Treaties Table
Discarded book covers, cherry plywood, glass
40"x24"x24"

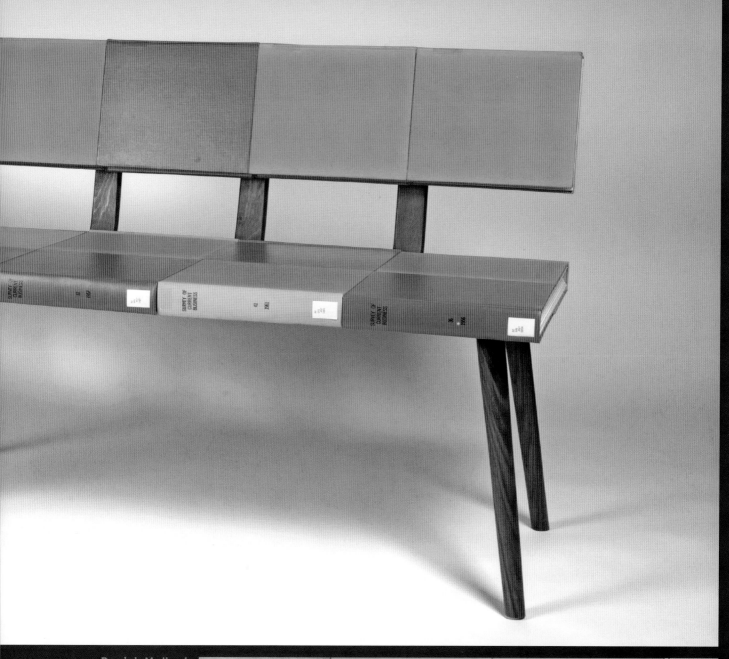

Derrick Method
SCR Bench
Walnut, bent ply lamination,
discarded book covers,
hardware
31.5" x 46"x25"

Andrew Pitts
Jewel Chest
Cherry, holly, red cedar, shellac polish, brass hardware
14"x8"x14"

Andrew Pitts
Pedestal Cabinet
Cherry, white oak, walnut, beech, shellac finish
38"x11"x11"

Christopher Poehlmann
Philadelphia, PA

Christopher Poehlmann
newGrowth Chandelier
Cherry, white oak, walnut,
beech, shellac finish
32"x18"x29"

Christopher Poehlmann
Stump Stool
Salvaged steel & wood
20"x20"x30"

Michael Puryear
Shokan, NY

Michael Puryear
Untitled chest
Bubinga, wenge
45"x32"x14"

Michael Puryear
Barrow Chair
Bubinga, leather
27.5"x29"x32"

Brian Reid
Rockland, ME

Brian Reid
The Quilted Chess Table
Solid maple, curly maple,
veneers of curly sycamore & curly maple
24" square x 27"
Photo by Dennis Griggs

Roy Rejean
Untitled table
Figured makore,
mahogany, black ebony
31"x39"x11"

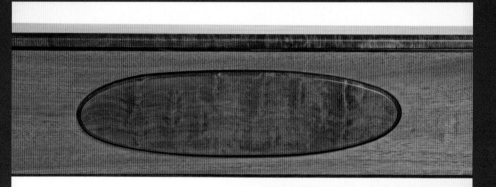

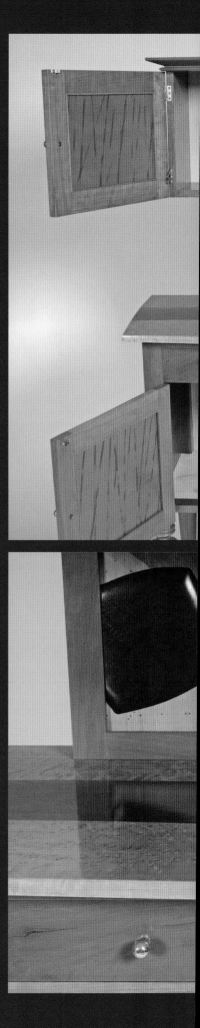

David Richardson
Views of the Hozu River
Cherry, painted and silk screened panel,
bird's eye maple and cherry
64"x42"x18"

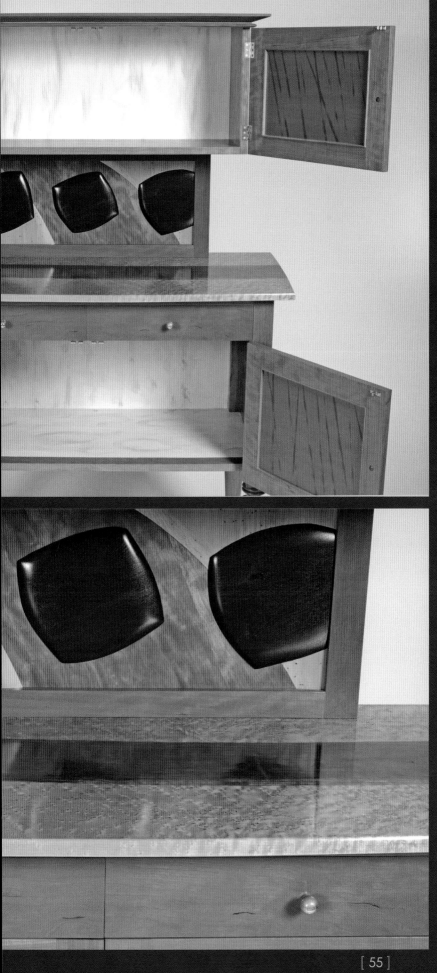

Cory Robinson
Indianapolis, IN

Cory Robinson
Tres Silhouette
Wood veneer, sandblasted acrylic
16" diameter x 24"

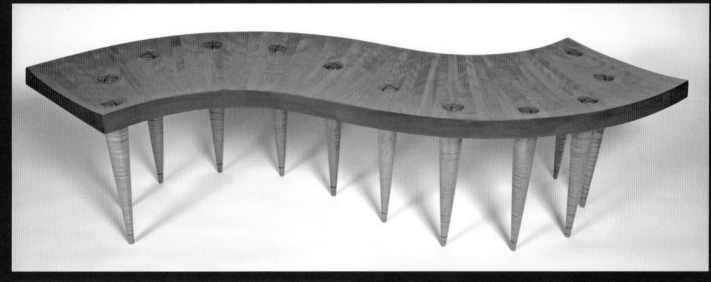

Mitch Ryerson
Cambridge, MA

Mitch Ryerson
River Bench
Flamed birch, curly maple, paint
17"x75"x18"

Mitch Ryerson
Matisse Chair
Maple, wenge, poplar, glaze, varnish, upholstery
19"x21"x34"

James Sagui
Double XXY-2
Basswood & special black metal leaf
5"x9"x26"

Paul Schurch
Manzanite High Table
Wanut, myrtle, tulipier,
elm, purpleheart,
mother-of-pearl, brass
34"x58"x43"

Alf Sharp
Side Table
Sapele, sycamore
13"x24"x21"

Jerry Spady
Air-acquarium
Claro walnut,
tiger maple, etim
32"x18"x60"

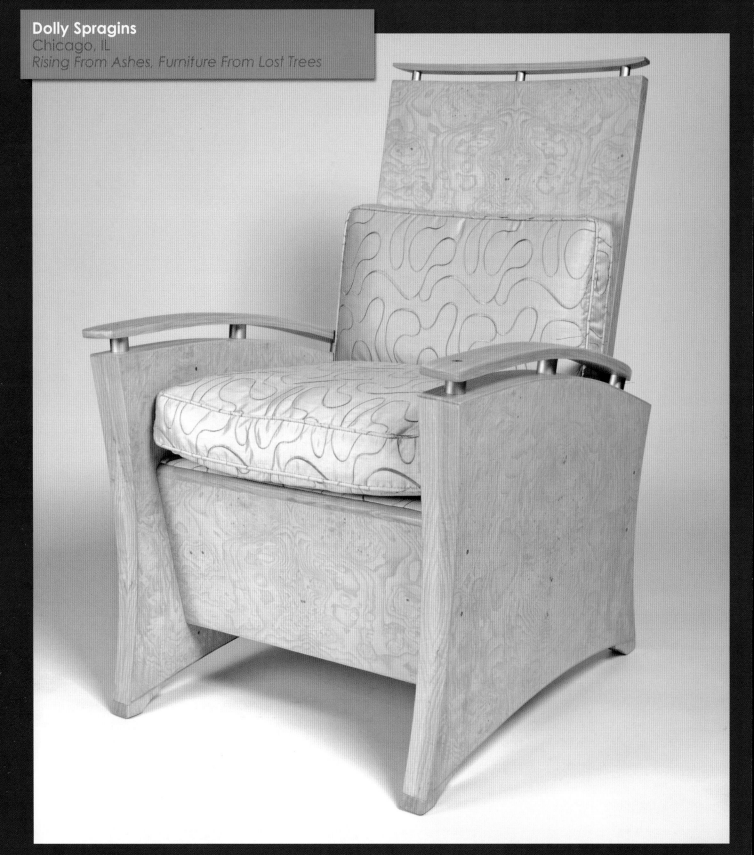

Dolly Spragins
Deco Chair
Ash burl veneer, plywood, aluminum, silk, down feathers
Photo: Stone 1

Kenneth J. Stone
Quilt frame
Commissioned for a Cambridge church,
where it is seen here installed; the frame
was used to hold the poster for the
conference. See page 9.

Allen Townsend
Andover, MA

Allen Townsend
Entry Table
Cherry, lacewood, wenge, varnish finish
29"x17.5"x17.5"

Robert Worth
Massachusetts College of Art and Design

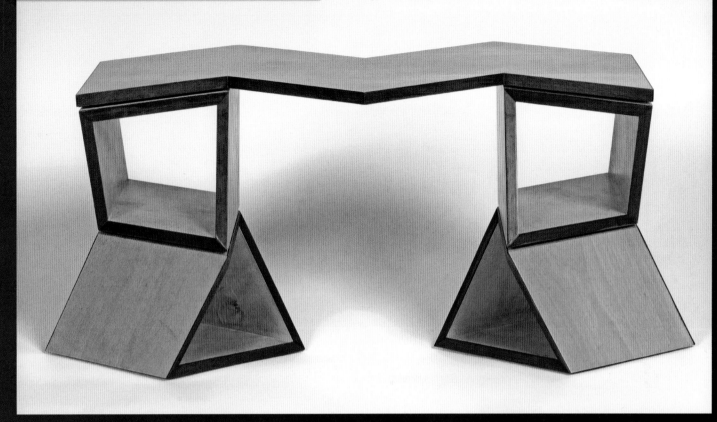

Robert Worth
Variations of Incomplete Open Cubes
Solid beech and walnut
29"x17.5"x17.5"

outdoor furniture: everyone is welcome

Mitch Ryerson

Artists were invited to submit proposals for an exhibit of outdoor furniture. The exhibit was located on the beautiful Kresge Green, between two buildings designed by Eero Saarinen in the heart of the MIT campus.

Jurors were Mark Del Guidice, a studio furniture maker and educator; Mitch Ryerson, a studio furniture maker and educator; Leah Woods, a studio furniture maker and faculty member of the University of New Hampshire; and Larry Sass, Assistant Professor of Computation, MIT Department of Architecture.

One might ask, "Why have an exhibit specifically for outdoor work by studio furniture makers?" In general, "outdoor furniture" conjures images of platoons of plastic lawn chairs, squadrons of folding metal chairs and battalions of "teakwood" benches. Lawn furniture, patio furniture, deck furniture; what self-respecting craftsperson would even want to go near this genre? Also, there is the miserable morass of "public seating." Mile upon mile of indestructible concrete and green 2' x 6' forms lining public walkways like so many dutiful drones offering a cold and impersonal embrace to the foot-weary populace! Surely, the skills and sensibilities of studio furniture makers can provide much needed relief and creativity.

Several years ago, with the help of an education grant from The Furniture Society, I took a trip to Paris to study public seating there. Although even the City of Light has its fair share of bad benches, I discovered a very different attitude and tradition surrounding the use of parks and seating in particular. Parks were really lived in. Fountains, cafés, boule courts, kiosks footpaths, and more created places where people were comfortable to hang out, relax, chat, read, kiss, etc., and what anchored the experience more than anything else was the seating. Lots and lots of seating. Benches in groups, benches alone, moveable chairs, seats in nooks or on overlooks, in the shade and in the sun. For the most part these were comfortable seats and functional seats. Seats that were not ashamed of being useful and also often very elegant. They were considered "important".

This was the basic premise for the "Everyone Is Welcome" exhibit. It proved that outdoor furniture truly is important and that it has great unexplored potential. The fifteen artists who exhibited in this show have ably demonstrated the truth in this. It takes a fair amount of nerve to take something so labor-intensive as a piece of handmade furniture and put it outside, exposed to the sun and rain, unprotected from all the people, dogs, and birds that pass it by. Yet there is also unique satisfaction in seeing how much enjoyment this furniture gives. People responded to it in a way seldom seen. They were puzzled [Why is it here?], intrigued [Can I sit on it?], and ultimately appreciative [This is so comfortable and cool!]. Not only can they touch the work, they really use it. This kind of adventurism by artists can happen in our cautious world, and when it does, it is appreciated

Technical issues with some pieces included problems with glues, finishes, wood movement, etc. When putting work outdoors there is no way to pretend it is durable if it is not. This exhibit posed the question and offered elegant and exciting responses.

Hayami Arakawa
West Newton, MA

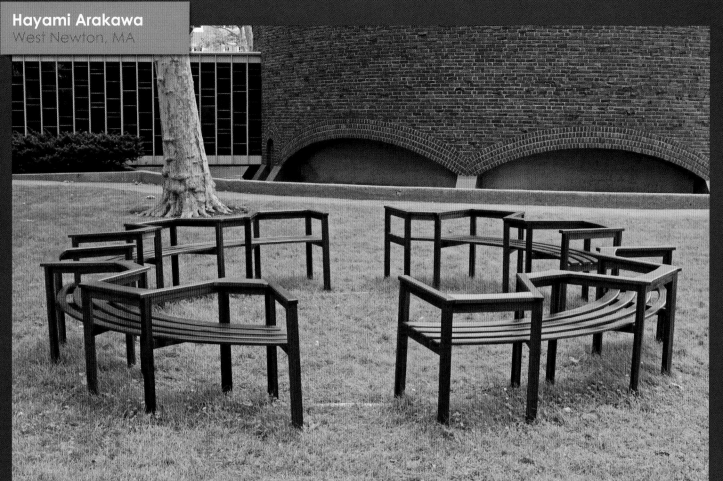

Hayami Arakawa
The Intellectuals' Circle

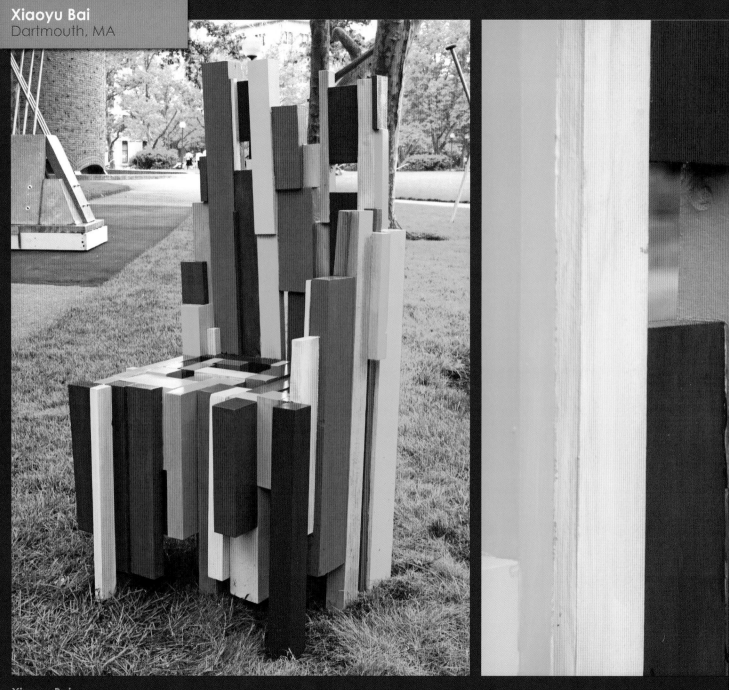

Xiaoyu Bai
Dartmouth, MA

Xiaoyu Bai
Colour Blocks

Dave Barresi
Pivoting Garden Bench

Frank Burns
Jamaica Plain, MA

Frank Burns
Lean Two
since 1991.

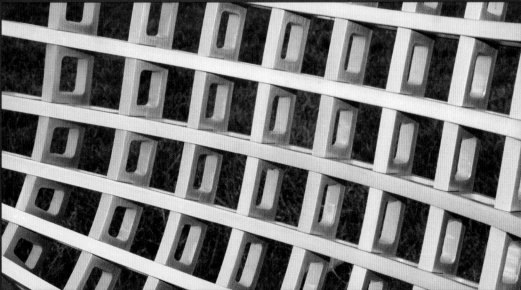

Stephen Iino
New York, NY

CONCEPT & DESIGN: Stephen Iino   INSTALLATION: Stephen Iino, Carol Sibley, Janet Lord and friends

Stephen Iino, Carol Sibley, Janet Lord
Knit Hammock, Knitting Needle Stand

Thomas Linville
Bronze Table

Judy Kensley McKie
Bird Tables

Robert Rickard
Conversation Bench

Peter Schelbecker
Kensington, MD

Peter Schelbecker
River Bench

Libby Schrum
Siblings

John Tagiuri
Somerville, MA

John Tagiuri
Lazy Hay

Robert Tiffany
Backless Bench

Joshua Torbick
Portsmouth, NH

Joshua Torbick
Observation Chair
sculpture

Horgato Zhou
Madison, WI

Horgato Zhou
Doggie Bone

six degrees of separation

Juried Exhibit

This juried exhibit of furniture featured artists who live in New England or graduated from a school in New England (Massachusetts, Connecticut, Rhode Island, Vermont, Maine, and New Hampshire). The exhibit was displayed in the Compton Gallery at MIT. Jurors were Miguel Gomez-Ibanez, furniture designer and maker, Past President of The Furniture Society, President of North Bennet Street School, Boston; Meredyth Hyatt Moses, art curator and former owner, Clark Gallery, Lincoln, Massachusetts; Tom Loeser, furniture maker, Professor, University of Wisconsin-Madison.

Jim Becker
Wilder, VT

Jim Becker
Foot Bowback Bench
Cherry, ash spindles, figured maple legs
60"x36.5"x21"

Ted Blachly
Ipanema Shaker Cupboard
White pine, white oak
27.25"x14.25"x62"

Tom Dahike
Bath, ME

Tom Dahike
Cunningham Fly Cabin
Silver maple, cherry, stone
24"x41"x38"

Mark Del Guidice
Adorn-meant
Makore, mahogany, basswood, milk paint
57"x18"x16"

Duncan Gowdy
Wall Cabinet with Pine Tree
Ash, maple, stain
27"x13"x6"

B.A. Harrington
Madison, WI

B.A. Harrington
Lineage
Quarter-sawn red oak, linseed oil, antique linens
36.25"x45"x19.5"
Courtesy of the Chipstone Foundation

Kyle Heffernan
Scottsdale, AZ

Kyle Heffernan
Tube Chair
Steel, nylon strapping
36"x36"x30"

Jacob Kulin
Coffee Table
Cedar, steel, glass
16"x20"x48"

Yoav Liberman
New York, NY

Yoav Liberman
Cantabrigian Highboy
Found plywood, found
specimen trays,
re-claimed walnut legs,
birch, maple, cherry

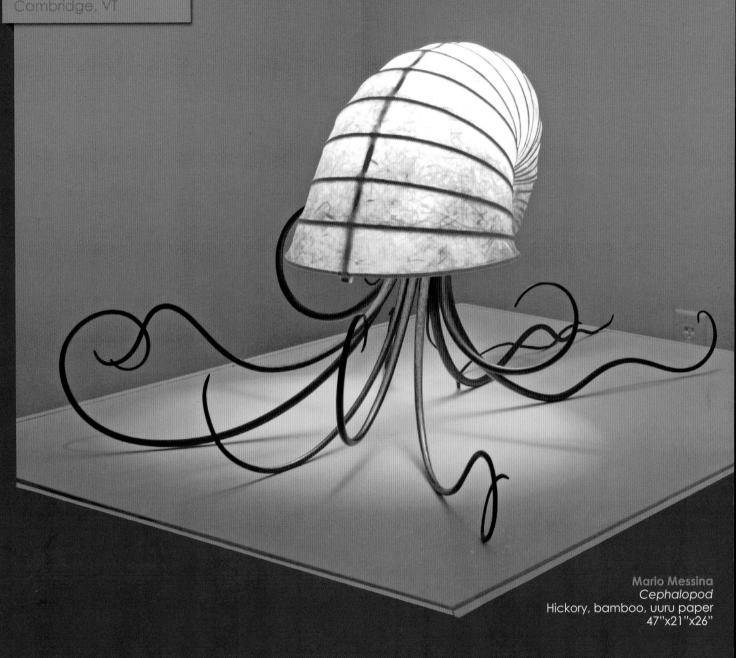

Mario Messina
Cephalopod
Hickory, bamboo, uuru paper
47"x21"x26"

Bart Niswonger
Textured Sideboard
Cherry frame, ash panels, paint
32"x66"x16"

Tim Nuanes
Bezel Table
Walnut, paldao
29"x51.5"x51.5"

James Sagui
West Palm Beach, FL

James Sagui
Until Next Year
Hand carved, bleached basswood
table 30"x30", chair 20"x27"x33"

Libby Schrum
Jewelry Box
Cherry, cherry burl, leather
8"x8"x16.5"

Thomas Shields
Support
Found chairs
47"x34"x41"
Collection of Memory Holloway

Jay Stanger
South Easton, MA

Jay Stanger
Finding Space
Dyed veneers, aluminum
19"x19"x72"

Rich Tannen
Tray
Maple
29"x6"x2"

William Thomas
Gaming Table
Mahogany, mahogany
& crotch birch veneers
30"x30"x20"

J.P. Vilkman
Portland, ME

J.P. Vilkman
Left: *K*
Wenge
21"x18"x20"

Right: *M*
White oak, walnut
24"x18"x18"

A. Thomas Walsh
West Stockbridge, MA

A. Thomas Walsh
Sleigh Endings Love Seat
Chilean tineo veneer,
solid mahogany base,
panaz green mohair
fabric, tung oil finish
61"x22"x22"

William E. Jewell

Historical Woods of America (HWA) has goals and services squarely focused on the reclamation, salvage, and creative re-purposing of historical trees and timbers, as well as trees from private, non-historic clients, such as homeowners with trees to which they have a sentimental connection. They work exclusively with trees that have fallen in storms, are diseased, unsafe, or being removed for construction, along with timbers removed from historical sites during renovation of existing structures.

HWA offers a historically significant, revenue-producing alternative to owners of historic trees. Instead of under-utilizing or discarding these limited, valuable resources at a landfill, they are committed to preserving history and the integrity of the environment through their unique services. Keenly focused on serving the general public in the mid-Atlantic area whose trees succumb to storms, are in decline, or are to be cleared for building purposes. They can turn their logs into flooring, architectural mill work, siding, furniture, lathe-turned art, or anything else wished for.

Garry Knox Bennett
Oakland, CA

Garry Knox Bennett
Post-Windsor Writing Chair
Thomas Jefferson's
Monticello tulip poplar,
ColorCore™, PVC, paint
30.75"x21"x28.25"

Michael Cullen
A Chest for a New Idea
Mount Vernon walnut, George Washington whiskey distillery walnut, milk paint
27.5"x11.75"x30.5"

Thomas Hucker
Washington Side Tables
George Washington whiskey
distillery walnut
24"x16"x24"

Thomas Hucker
"Dearest Sally" Writing Chair
George Washington
whiskey distillery walnut
with marquetry
20"x20"x32"

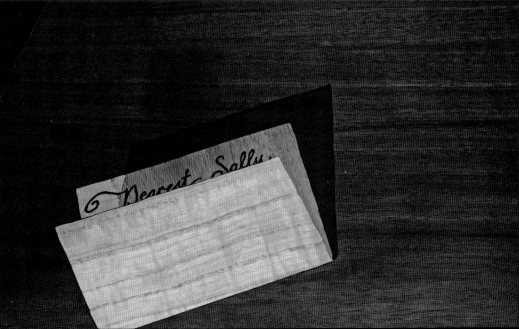

William E. Jewell
Woodford, VA

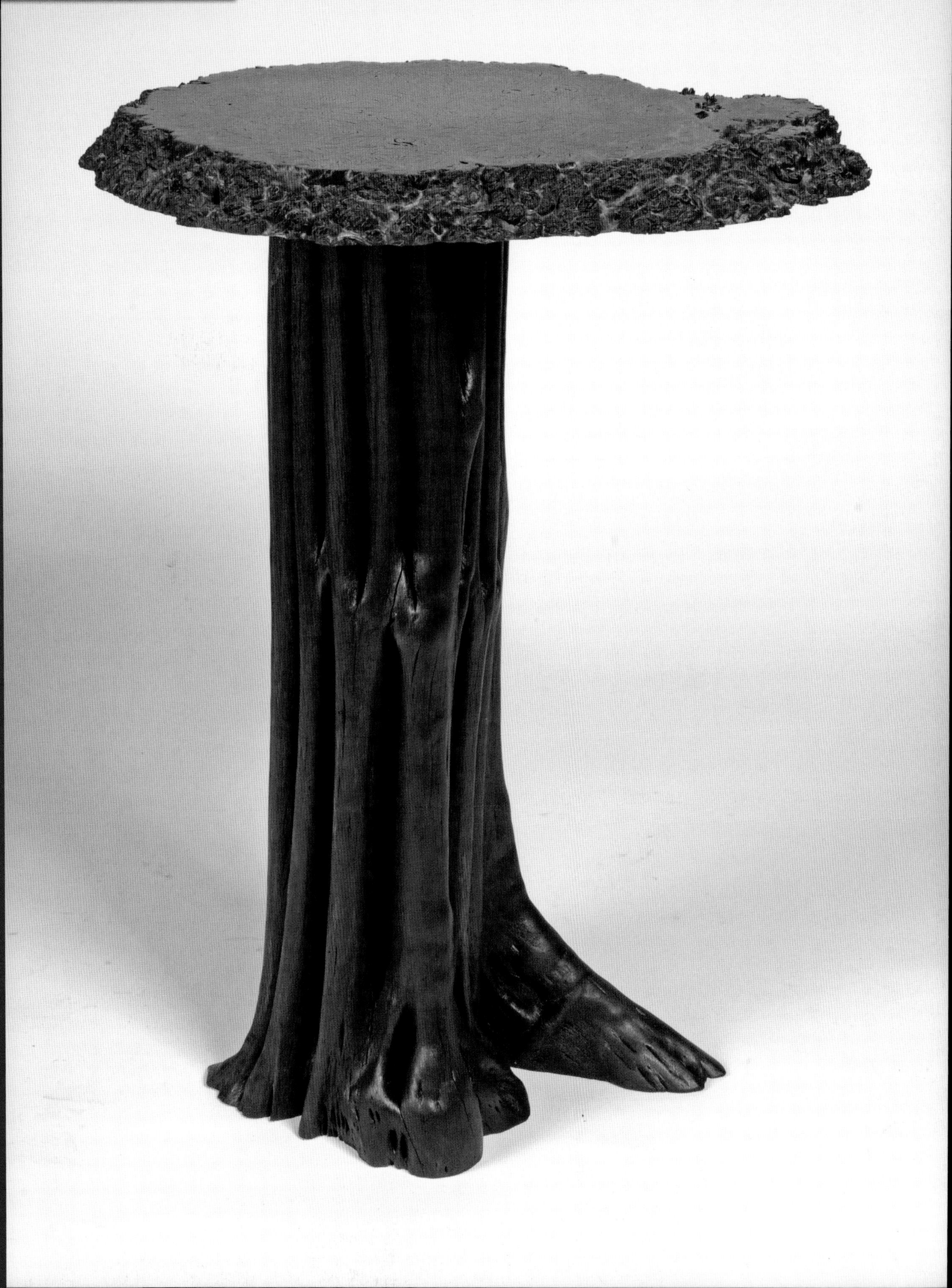

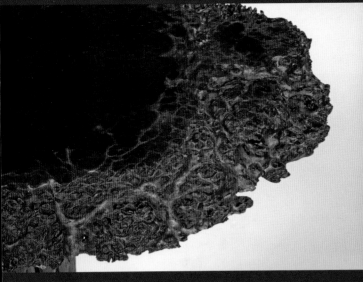
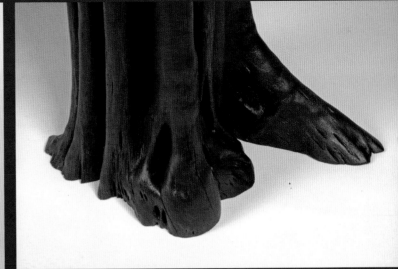

William E. Jewell
Connected
Jarrah burl, Australia,
Saguaro cactus skeleton,
Sonora Desert
22"x34"

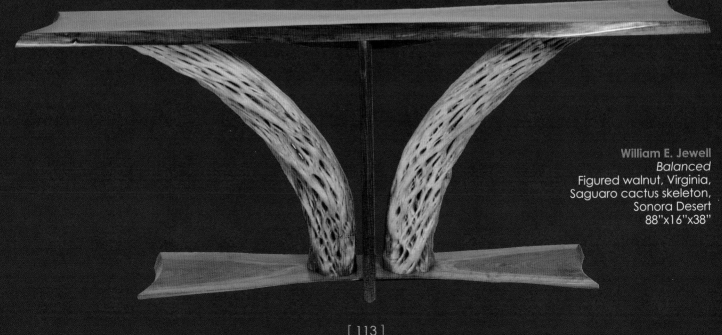

William E. Jewell
Balanced
Figured walnut, Virginia,
Saguaro cactus skeleton,
Sonora Desert
88"x16"x38"

Silas Kopf
Founding Fathers Writing Desk
George Washington whiskey distillery walnut with marquetry, using 15 historic woods
52"x22"x30"

Wendy Maruyama
San Diego, CA

Wendy Maruyama
Fractured
Thomas Jefferson's Monticello
American elm 85"x12"x15"

Brian Newell with Jason Newell
Scroll Case
James Monroe boxwood & James Madison cedar of Lebanon
21.5""x6.5"x7.5"

Student Works

"Faculty Selects" is an annual showcase of student work nominated for exhibition by faculty members. Submissions are juried by a panel consisting of the current Student Representative to The Furniture Society Board of Trustees and two or more selected educators. The work was published in *Furniture Studio* (volumes 3, 4, and 5), and in 2008 the exhibit was converted to an online catalog. Works in 2010 were exhibited in the Kresge Auditorium lobby at MIT.

Faculty of all furniture programs—non-matriculating, undergraduate or graduate—were encouraged to nominate their students' best work for this exhibition. Jurors were Chris Schwab, Tom Loeser and Alan Harp.

Jon Bonser
San Diego State University

Jon Bonser
Sacastry chair
Wenge, ebony, leather upholstery
San Diego State University

Luc Collette
Wizard's Precedent
Maine College of Art

Ray Duffey
Shell Stool
Herron School
of Art and Design

Ray Duffey
Herron School of Art and Design

David Hancock
Boston Bombe
North Bennet Street School

Adam John Manley
San Diego State University

Adam John Manley
Adrift (San Diego pool)
Cypress, steel plates, hardware
7'x45"
San Diego State University

Austin McAdams
Virginia Commonwealth University

Austin McAdams
Pinch Dog Bench
Virginia Commonwealth
University

Greg McIlvaine
Kutztown University of Pennsylvania

Greg McIlvaine
Something To Sit On
Kutztown University of Pennsylvania

Trevor Ritchie
Rochester Institute of Technology School for American Crafts

Trevor Ritchie
Table
Rochester Institute of
Technology School for
American Crafts

Ashley Robinson
Herron School of Art and Design

Ashley Robinson
Classic Showoffs
Herron School of Art and Design

David Trees
North Bennet Street School

Devon Trom
Virginia Commonwealth University

Devon Trom
Pierced Lamp
Virginia Commonwealth University

Heather Trosdahl
Ripple
College of the Redwoods

George Tsai
Elika Table
Massachusetts Institute of Technology

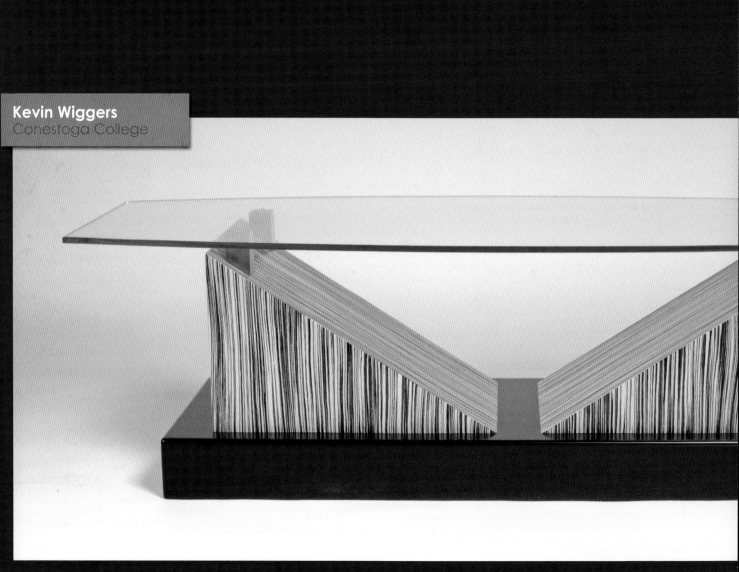

Kevin Wiggers
Levee Table
Conestoga College

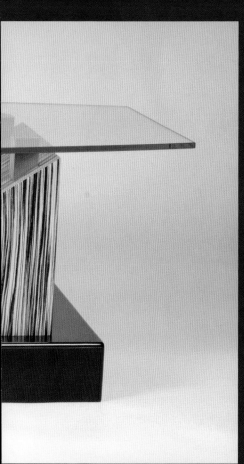

Robert Worth
The Hive
Massachusetts College of Art and Design

The Furniture Society Members & Guest Exhibitors

A

Agnes Bourne Studio
Agnes Bourne
PO Box 3797
2190 N Elk Refuge Rd.
Jackson, WY 83011-3797
307.699.0708

Robert Aibel,
see Moderne Gallery

Al McClain Woodworking
Al McClain
10 N Main St.
Kent, CT 06757
WWW.ALMCCLAIN.COM

Laron Algren
6363 N Dayton-
Lakeview Rd.
New Carlisle, OH 45344
WWW.LARONALGREN.COM

Joshua Almond
Department of Art
and Art History
1000 Holt Ave.
Winter Park, FL 32789
WWW.JOSHALMOND.COM

Jerry Alonzo
28 Cavalry Rd.
Geneseo, NY 14454
585.243.1147

Joe Amaral
PO Box 614
Fort Bragg, CA 95437
WWW.WOODFINISHSERVICES.COM

John Amdall
901 Wellington
Washington, IL 61571-1376
309.444.5602

Jeffrey Amer
14 Calvin Ave.
Syosset, NY 11791
516.682.0555

Jonathan Amson
1504 S Stafford St.
Arlington, VA 22204

Om Anand
PO Box 2999
Santa Cruz, CA 95063
831.479.3590

Jennifer Anderson
4559 Bermuda Ave.
San Diego, CA 92107
619.846.6139

Reid Anderson
400 Melrose Ave. #604
Seattle, WA 98102

Anthony Van Dunk
Woodworker
Anthony Jay Van Dunk
63 Fort Greene Pl. 20
Brooklyn, NY 11217

Hayami Arakawa
85 Eliot Ave.
Newton, MA

Anatevka Arguezo
9104 Brightleaf Pl.
Charlotte, NC 28269

Michael Aronson
1179 Hymettus Ave.
Leucadia, CA 92024

Art Beyond Borders
Mechthild Wagner
164 Blvd.
Scarsdale, NY 10583
917-713-4494
WWW.ARTBEYONDBORDERS.COM

Artful Inventions
by Aren Irwin
Aren Irwin
333 Pueblo Solano Rd. NW
Los Ranchos, NM 87107
505.333.8242
WWW.ARTFULINVENTIONS.COM

Tyson Atwell
342 Ohio St.
Vallejo, CA 94590
WWW.TYSONATWELL.COM

Teresa Audet
2420 Blaisdell Ave. S
Minneapolis, MN 55404

Zaid Auzam
Sheridan College
Oakville, ON L6J7T8
Canada

B

Lee Badger
101 Potato Hill
PO Box 1313
Hedgesville, WV 25427
304.754.3282
WWW.ANVILWORKS.NET

Xiaoyu Bai
22 Old Westport Road
Dartmouth, MA 02747

Dawn Baker
242 Sheboygan St.
Fond Du Lac, WI 54935

Russell Baldon
943 42nd St.
Oakland, CA 94608
415.505.8990
WWW.RUSSELLBALDON.
POSTEROUS.COM

Boris Bally
789 Atwells Ave.
Providence, RI 02909

Joyce Barker-Schwartz
8221 Fairview Rd.
Elkins Park, PA 19027
215.236.0745
WWW.JBSDESIGNS.NET

David Barresi
9679 Center Rd.
Traverse City, MI 49686
231.492.4139
WWW.STYLEBYDESIGN.BIZ

Carl Bass
47 Oakvale Ave.
Berkeley, CA 94705

Sam Batchelor
881 E First St. #305
S. Boston, MA 02127
617.894.1714

Keith Battersby
1793 Dean Park Rd.
North Saanich, BC V8L1B9
Canada
250.655.7029

Gregory Bauer
67 Mcelderry Rd.
Guelph, ON N1G 4J2
Canada

Joe Bauman
Sheridan College
Oakville, ON L6J7T8
Canada

Troy Beall,
*see The School at
Annapolis Woodworks*

Lee Beatrous
5500 Lockridge Rd.
Durham, NC 27705

James (Jim) Becker
45 A St. Commerce Park
PO Box 802
Wilder, VT 05088

Susan Beckerman
32 W 88th St.
New York, NY 10024
212.724.4351

Chris Becksvoort
PO Box 12
New Gloucester, ME
  04260
207.926.4608
WWW.CHBECKSVOORT.COM

Max Beelaerts Van
  Blokland
Sheridan College
Oakville, ON L6J7T8
Canada

Vivian Beer
21 Dow Street
Manchester, NH 03101
845.239.2729
WWW.VIVIANBEER.COM

Dorothy Leigh Bell
1172 Dean St.
Brooklyn, NY 11216

Mark Bench
200 West 93rd Street # 5G
New York, NY 10025
917-628-4692

Garry Knox Bennett
130 Fourth St.
Oakland, CA 94607
510.465.5637
WWW.GKB-FURNITURE.COM

Robert Bennett
PO Box 846
Freeland, WA 98249-0846
RHBFURNITUREMAKER.COM

Sylvia Bennett
130 Fourth St.
Oakland, CA 94607
510.465.5637

Jan Benson
1883 Vinsetta Blvd.
Royal Oak, MI 48073

Gill Benzion
Sheridan College
Oakville, ON L6J7T8
Canada

Larry Berger
227 Trevarno Rd.
Livermore, CA 94551

Robert Bergman
4943 S Woodlawn Ave.
Chicago, IL 60615
773.285.8420

Darren Bertuccio
665 Pine St.
Victoria, BC V9A 2Z9
Canada
250.213.7795

Nigel Best
PO Box 143
Calhoun, MO 65323

Eckhard Bez
67 Sunset Ridge Ln.
Bolton, MA 01740

Timothy G. Biggs
279 Sterling Pl., #1A
Brooklyn, NY 11238

Ted Blachly
PO Box 216
Warner, NH 03278
WWW.TEDBLACHLY.COM

Elise Black
19A Darbrook Rd.
Westport, CT 06880

Juan Pablo Blanco
56 Columbus St
Newton Highlands, MA
  02461

Eben Blaney
96 Eddy Rd.
PO Box 408
Edgecomb, ME 04556

Jake Blok
5942 W N Ave.
Kalamazoo, MI 49009
WWW.JBLOKSTUDIOS.COM

Roslyn Bock,
  see Sam Maloof
  Woodworker, Inc.

Stephen Bodner
689 Fearrington Post
Pittsboro, NC 27312

Dan Bollock
12 N 28th St.
Lafayette, IN 47904
WWW.DANBOLLOCK.COM

Robert Bonham
1220 Poplar St.
Lebanon, PA 17042

Anne Bossert
1624 S Whitcomb St.
Fort Collins, CO 80526
970.988.9503

Agnes Bourne, see Agnes
  Bourne Studio

Kevin Bowen
3051 Bay Shore Dr.
Orchard Lake, MI 48324
248.682.4015

Winston Bowen
15340 Seadrift Ave. Box 94
Caspar, CA 95420

Christina Boy
191 C Belleview Ave
Orange, VA 22960
WWW.CHRISTINABOY.COM

Boykin Pearce Associates
Dave Boykin
1875 E 27th Ave.
Denver, CO 80205-4527
303.294.0703
WWW.BOYKINPEARCE.COM

Bruce Bradford
763 Barnsdale Rd.
Winston Salem, NC 27106
336.692.1092
WWW.BRADFORDCUSTOMFURNITURE.
  COM

Bradford Woodworking
Brad Smith
PO Box 157
3120 Fisher Rd.
Worcester, PA 19490
610.584.1150

Alan Bradstreet
856 Lawrence Rd.
Pownal, ME 04069
207.688.4728

Robert Bragg
14328 Cricket Ln.
Abingdon, VA 24210
276.451.0417

Peter Braham
715 N. Nelson St.
Arlington, VA 22203-2214

Timothy Brauer
1081 S Clarkson St.
Denver, CO 80209
303.315.2071

Scott Braun
361 Stagg St. # 14
Brooklyn, NY 11206

BRC Designs
Benjamin Rollins Caldwell
124 Lake Bowen Dr.
Inman, SC 29349

Doug Brill,
*see Doug Brill Artistic
Woodworking*

Garner Britt
111 Hawk Terrace
Vilas, NC 28692

Dane Broe
Sheridan College
Oakville, ON L6J7T8
Canada

Michael Brolly
1405 Chelsea Ave.
Bethlehem, PA 18018
613.332.5376

Garrett Brooks
42 Division Ave S
Grand Rapids, MI 49503

Jon Brooks
81 Pine Rd.
New Boston, NH 03070
603.487.2780
WWW.JONBROOKS.ORG

Kevin Bross
29 Plant St.
Cumberland, RI 02864

Robert Brou
1564 Dekalb Ave. #5
Atlanta, GA 30307
WWW.NATURALISMFURNITURE.COM

Barbara Brown
6 Avondale St.
Dorchester, MA 02124

Gail Brown
53 N. Mascher St. #2 R/2F
Philadelphia, PA 19106
215.925.6017

Greg Brown
1589 1st NH Turnpike
Northwood, NH 03261
WWW.GBWOODWORKS.COM

Michael Brown
670 Howell Rd.
Grantsboro, NC 28529
252.249.1348

Richard Bubnowski
807 Bradley Rd.
Point Pleasant Beach,
   NJ 08742
732.701.4900
WWW.RICHARDBUBNOWSKIDESIGN.
   COM

David Buchanan
650 W Washington St.
Indianapolis, IN 46204
317.509.9215
WWW.INDIANAMUSEUM.ORG

Larry Buechley
El Valle Rte. Box 21
Chamisal, NM 87521
505.689.2445
WWW.BUECHLEYWOODWORKING.
   COM

Nancy Buechley
El Valle Rte. Box 21
Chamisal, NM 87521
505.689.2445

Kenneth Bures
16 Washington Sq.
Marblehead, MA 01945

David Burling
145 Bishop Lamy Rd.
Lamy, NM 87540
505.466.8011

Frank Burns
38 Greenough Ave.
Jamaica Plain, MA 02130
617.524.2676

Moshe Bursuker
4 Park Way
Pur, NY 10578

Jeffrey Burt
Sheridan College
Oakville, ON L6J7T8
Canada

Geoff Burton
2928 Blackwood St.
Victoria, BC V8T 3X2
Canada

Todd Butler
3851 NE Campus Ln.
Bremerton, WA 98311
WWW.THEBUTLERDIDIT.WS

Corwin Butterworth,
*see Corwin Butterworth
Custom Furniture*

Benjamin Rollins Caldwell,
see BRC Designs

David Calvin
1405 N Lorraine Ave.
Muncie, IN 47304
765.286.4126

John Cameron
34 Mt. Pleasant Ave. #5
Gloucester, MA 01930
978.283.0276

Graham Campbell
1560 Craft Center Dr.
Smithville, TN 37166
615.597.6801

Arlene Caplan
466 Southern Blvd.
Chatham, NJ 07928

Miriam Carpenter
513 Hillcrest Ave.
Morrisville, PA 19067

Nicole Carroll
46 Longyear Rd.
Shokan, NY 12481
845.943.5975

Jeff Carter, *see The
Westmount Group*

Steve Casey
5560 Fairview Pl.
Agoura Hills, CA 91301
818.706.3147
WWW.STEVECASEYDESIGN.COM

Victoriano Castaneda
7 Depot Ct. #3
Cohasset, MA 02025

Wendell Castle
18 Maple St.
Scottsville, NY 14546
585.889.2378

Cerca Trova Design
Matthew Shively
1150 Hughes Ln.
Lexington, KY 40511

Rob Chamberlin
610 Rose St.
Kalamazoo, MI 49007

Juston Chan
Sheridan College
Oakville, ON L6J7T8
Canada

Chris Charuk
Sheridan College
Oakville, ON L6J7T8
Canada

Colin Chase
Chase Sculpture Studios
26 S Partition St.
Saugerties, NY 12477

Robert Chen
Sheridan College
Oakville, ON L6J7T8
Canada

Steven Chisholm
11 Wheeler Pl. NW
Edmonton, AB T6M 2E7
Canada

Kip Christensen
Brigham Young University
230 Snell Bldg.
Provo, UT 84602-4206

William Clark
555 Saturn Blvd. B-653
San Diego, CA 92154

Don Clarke
321 Quail Run
Anderson, SC 29621

Ed Clay
5398 Carneros Hwy.
Napa, CA 94559
707.224.3169
WWW.EDCLAY.COM

Stephen Clerico
PO Box 192
Free Union, VA 22940
434.978.4109
WWW.STEPHENCLERICO.COM

Gerry Clifford
90 Sandy Valley Rd.
Dedham, MA 02026
781.329.0850

William Clinton
160 Cheever Hall
Bozeman, MT 59717
406.994.4402

Todd Clippinger
15 Garden Ave.
Billings, MT 59101

Keith Cochran
402 5th St. SW
Fort Payne, AL 35967
WWW.WOODSTUDIO.COM

Randy and Dylan
   Cochran, see Wood
   Studio

Jim Coffey
3663 54 Ave.
Innisfail, AB T4G 1E7
Canada
403.350.6324
WWW.JIMCOFFEY.CA

Warren Cole
518 N Bragg Ave.
Lookout Mountain,
   TN 37350

Robert Coles
17 Derby Rd.
Port Washington, NY 11050
WWW.BELWOODNY.COM

College of the Redwoods
440 Alger St.
Fort Bragg, CA 95437
707.964.7056
WWW.CRFINEFURNITURE.COM

Carrie Compton
709 Quincy St. SE
Albuquerque, NM 87108

Brian Condran
12 Dickson Ln.
Martinez, CA 94553
925.372.8171

Martha Connell
158 Rumson Rd.
Atlanta, GA 30305
404.261.1712

Shawn Connor
3971 Green St.
Harrisburg, PA 17110
WWW.CONNORARTISTRY.COM

Ernie Conover
PO Box 679
18115 Madison Rd.
Parkman, OH 44062
WWW.CONOVERWORKSHOPS.COM

Edward Cooke, Jr.
26 Lowell Ave.
Newtonville, MA 02460
617.965.7154

Paula Cooperrider
8925 W Longmeadow Dr.
Prescott, AZ 86305
928.899.5784

John Corcoran
70 Hollenbeck Ave.
Great Barrington,
   MA 01230

Donald Corey
919 Brookside Dr.
Raleigh, NC 27604

Corwin Butterworth
   Custom Furniture
Corwin Butterworth
34 Cleveland St.
Wakefield, RI 02879-3306
401.440.2798

Jennifer Costa
203 Clayton Ct.
East Peoria, IL 61611
309.698.6223
WWW.JENNIFERCOSTASTUDIO.COM

Bettie Cott
1430 Trafalgar Rd.
Oakville, ON L6H 2L1
Canada

Dale Cox
8799 Featherleigh Ln.
Germantown, TN 38138

CP Lighting
Christopher Poehlmann
3201 Fox St.
Philadelphia, PA 19129
866.597.4800
WWW.CPLIGHTING.COM

Richard Crangle
30 Bennett St. N
Gloucester, MA 01930

John Crawford
27 Cherry St.
Arden, NC 28704

Kyle Crawford
210 E Hersey St.
PO Box 730
Ashland, OR 97520

Kenneth Creed
10 E End Ave. #4D
New York, NY 10075

Frederic Crist
South River Complex
200 W 12th St.
Waynesboro, VA 22980
540.942.7854
WWW.FACRISTMETALSMITH.COM

Thomas Crosby
528 Park Ave.
Whitefish, MT 59937

Erika Cross
336 S Division, Apt. 10
Ann Arbor, MI 48104

Michael Cullen
500 Rohde Lane
Petaluma, CA 94952
WWW.MICHAELCULLENDESIGN.COM

Matthew Curry
13780 Silven Ave. NE
Bainbridge Island,
   WA 98110
323.463.1101
WWW.MSCDESIGN.COM

Kevin Cwalina
77 Bradley St.
Asheville, NC 28806

Mark Cwik
1965 W Pershing Rd. #A6
Chicago, IL 60609
773.750.7725
WWW.MARKCWIKSTUDIO.COM

Gary Daab
PO Box 37842
Jacksonville, FL 32236
904.610.2569
WWW.VERDANT-DESIGNS.COM

Tom Dahlke
2 Anchor Rd.
Bath, ME 04530
207.443.2108
WWW.NORTHFORKWOODWORKS.
   COM

John Dale
1800 Valley Ridge Rd.
Norman, OK 73072

Dapwood Furniture
Gregg Mich
3303 Vassar Dr. NE
Albuquerque, NM 87107

Kate Davidson
3613 Richardt Ave.
Evansville, IN 47715

Jeff Davis
560 Kellogg St.
Plymouth, MI 48170

dbO Home
Daniel Oates
PO Box 626
Sharon, CT 06069

Michael de Forest
12275 NW Old Quarry Rd.
Portland, OR 97229-4735
503.297.5544, x192
WWW.MICHAELDEFORESTSTUDIO.
   COM

David de Muzio
110 Llanfair Rd.
Cynwyd, PA 19004-2812
215.684.7555

Bruce Delaney,
   see WSS Design, LLC

Mark Del Guidice,
   see Mark Del Guidice
   Furniture Maker

Sybil Delgaudio
201 E 19 St. 5D
New York, NY 10003

David Delthony
PO Box 437,
1540 W Hwy 12
Escalante, UT 84726-0437
435.826.4631

Ted Demers
66 Mirtl Rd.
PO Box 292
Willington, CT 06279-0292
860.429.7267
WWW.EVERLASTINGWOODS.COM

Donna DeMott
9734 Twin Creek Dr.
Dallas, TX 75228

Ellen Denker
PO Box 1532
Burnsville, NC 28714-1532

Donald Denmeade
7782 Tackabury Rd.
Canastota, NY 13032
315.247.8013
WWW.DENMEADEFWW.COM

Larry Denning
2109 Coral Dr.
Arlington, TX 76010
817.456.8441

John Dennison
2000 Bazan Bay Rd.
North Saanich, BC V8T 5K3
Canada

Arnold d'Epagnier
14201 Notley Rd.
Colesville, MD 20904
301.384.3201

Chris Derven
306 Piermont Ave.
Piermont, NY 10968
845.365.0420

Christopher Dewart
336 Norfolk St. Apt 1
Cambridge, MA 02139

Forest Dickey
170 Parnassus Ave. #6
San Francisco, CA 94117
WWW.VARIANDESIGNS.COM

Rob Diemert
1430 Trafalgar Rd.
Oakville, ON L6H 2L1
Canada
905.845.9430, x2659
WWW1.SHERIDANINSTITUTE.CA

Mark Dillon
909 Myers Ave.
Columbia, TN 38401
931.380.5597
WWW.MARKDILLONDESIGNS.COM

Arthur Dion,
  see Gallery NAGA

Jack Dodds
2048 Kaiser Rd.
Galien, MI 49113
269.545.8801

Trevor Doig
6312 - 43A Ave.
Camrose, AB T4V 3N3
Canada

Donovan Furniture Studio
Rod Donovan
18192 E Adriatic Pl.
Aurora, CO 80013
WWW.RODDONOVAN.COM

Steffanie Dotson
1054 Devonshire Dr.
San Diego, CA 92107
858.354.8853
WWW.STEFFANIEDOTSON.COM

William Doub
63 Nottingham Rd.
Deerfield, NH 03037
603.463.8992
WWW.CUSTOMFURNITURE-DOUB.
  COM

Doug Brill Artistic
  Woodworking
Doug Brill
51 Cedar Lane
Jamestown, RI 02835

Downsworks
Martha Downs
3979 Hwy JJ
Black Earth, WI 53515
608.767.3094
WWW.DOWNSWORKS.COM

Laura Drake
418 W Main St.
Crawfordsville, IN 47933

Art Drauglis
2507 Queens
  Chapel Rd. NE
Washington, DC 20018
202.679.0066

Derrick Du Toit
15 Cedargrove Ct.
Ottawa, ON K2G 0M4
Canada
613.820.6743

Craig DuBose
1066 Old Lynchburg Rd.
Charlottesville, VA 22903
434.977.8439

Ray Duffey
555 Woodruff Place
  Middle Dr.
Indianapolis, IN 46201

Ralph Duncan
PO Box 3465
Silverdale, WA 98383

Syd Dunton
22425 Summit Rd.
Los Gatos, CA 95033
408.353.4731

Chris Dutch
713 White Oak Rd.
Charleston, WV 25302
304.344.8847

LindaSue Eastman
24004 Homer Valley Rd.
Winona, MN 55987
507.454.7435

David Ebner
5 Newey Ln.
Brook Haven, NY 11719
631.286.4523
WWW.DAVIDNEBNER.COM

Sheila Edwards
114 W 41St St.
Savannah, GA 31401

Carley Eisenberg
2048 Laguna Way
Naples, FL 34109

Paul Eisenhauer
821 W Bridge St.
Phoenixville, PA 19460

Timothy Ellsworth,
  see Roskear
  Fine Furniture

Ariel Enriquez
6007 N Villard Ave.
Portland, OR 97217

Paul Epp
12 Huron St.
Toronto, ON M5T 2A1
Canada
416.804.4702
WWW.PAULEPP.COM

Robert Erickson,
  see Robert Erickson
  Woodworking

Karen Ernst
Edinboro University of PA
113 Doucette Hall, Art
  Department
Edinboro, PA 16444
814.732.2588
WWW.ART.EDINBORO.EDU/
  PROGRAMS

Emeka Ezerioha
Suite A15B Bobsar
  Complex Area 11 Garki
Fct, 2349
Nigeria

Ken Faber
2163 S Fillmore St.
Denver, CO 80210

Bob Fain
1821 Meadow Lark Dr.
Flagstaff, AZ 86001
928.779.1167

Jonathan Fairbanks
247 Nahatan St.
Westwood, MA 02090
781.329.3098

Seamus Fairtlough
43-01 21st St. Suite 304B
Long Island City, NY 11101

Tom Fama
25 Hutchinson Dr.
Marlborough, MA 01752
508.480.9762

Richard Farwell
2129 Fairchild Way #1B
PO Box 6422
Los Osos, CA 93412-6422
805.528.5528
WWW.LOSOSOSWOODWORKING.
  COM

Robert Fergerson
3000 Cathedral Ave. NW
Washington, DC 20008
202.939.8836

Ross Fiersten
2215 S. Union Ave, 406
Chicago, IL 60616
312.563.9621
WWW.RFMETALWORKS.COM

Raymond Finan
PO Box 189
Arlington, VT 05250
802.681.5393
WWW.RAYMONDFINAN.COM

Fine Furnishings Shows
Karla Little
80 Main Rd. # 203
Tiverton, RI 02878
401.816.0963

Fine Wood Artists /
  Nakisha.com
Nakisha VanderHoeven
9032 Renton Ave. S
Seattle, WA 98118

Fine Woodworking
  Magazine
63 S Main St. - PO Box 5506
Newtown, CT 06470-5506
203.304.3417
WWW.FINEWOODWORKING.COM

Mark Finnigan
Sheridan College
Oakville, ON L6J7T8
Canada

Brian Fireman
122 Vineyard Rd.
Tryon, NC 28782
828.712.6660

Irving Fischman
106 Summer St.
Somerville, MA 02143
617.628.6515

Howard Fisher
5 Via Vaquera
Carmel, CA 93923
831.625.1836

Paige Fissel
7651 Cornell Rd.
Montgomery, OH 45242

Dennis FitzGerald
12 Tower Hill Rd.
Pawling, NY 12564
914.251.6763

Oscar Fitzgerald
206 W Monroe Ave.
Alexandria, VA 22301

Mike Flaim
1260 Kent Dr.
Milford, OH 45150
WWW.MVFLAIM.COM

David Fleming
5302 E Nisbet Rd.
Scottsdale, AZ 85254
602.308.9188
WWW.DFCABINETMAKER.COM

Peter Fleming
1430 Trafalgar Rd.
Oakville, ON L6H 2L1
Canada
905.845.9430, x2659

J. Michael Floyd
810 W 9th St.
Cookeville, TN 38501
931.526.1583

Reuben Foat
4717 Felton St.
San Diego, CA 92116

Mats Fogelvik
PO Box 377475
Ocean View, HI 96737
808.280.8405
WWW.FOGELVIK.COM

Richard Ford, Jr.
5179 Diane Ln.
Livermore, CA 94550
619.607.2772

Amy Forsyth
21 Merkle Rd.
Bechtelsville, PA 19505
610.845.9779

Michael Fortune
1623 English Line RR #2
Lakefield, ON K0L 2H0
Canada
705.652.0037

John Foster
78 Pleasant St.
Hopkinton, MA 01748
508.435.6679
WWW.FOSTERCUSTOMFURNITURE.
  COM

Kamal Fox
Sheridan College
Oakville, ON L6J7T8
Canada

Jonathan Francis
165 Forest St.
Wellesley, MA 02481

Jason Frantz
1303 E Cambridge
Springfield, MO 65804
1.866.615.3416

David Fraser,
  see Michael Grace/
  David Fraser Fine
  Woodworking Dept.

Diana Frazier
2029 Enslow Blvd.
Huntington, WV 25701

Gail Fredell
156A Cumberland Ave.
Asheville, NC 28801
WWW.GAILFREDELL.COM

Samantha Freeman
1204 N Lawrence St.
Philadelphia, PA 19122

Richard Frinier,
  see Richard
  Frinier Collection

Claire Fruitman
PO Box 157
Williamsburg, MA 01096
617.216.6791

Rachel Fuld
315 Cherry St.
Philadelphia, PA 19106
267.235.8926

Mike Fulop
405 18th St. W
Saskatoon, SK s7m 1c7
Canada

Paul Fussell
3496 Peachtree Pkwy #B1
Suwanee, GA 30024
678.965.4016
WWW.THEINNOVATIVEWOOD.COM

▬▬◄G►▬▬

Gallery NAGA
Arthur Dion
67 Newbury St.
Boston, MA 02116
617.267.9060

Robert Galusha
PO Box 92771
Austin, TX 78709
WWW.ROBERTGALUSHADESIGN.COM

Paula Garbarino
574 Boston Ave. # 403
Medford, MA 02155

Bill Garbus
Arcisan Studio
125 Weed St.
New Canaan, CT 06840
203.981.7653
WWW.ARCISAN.COM

Lizeth Garcia
221 E 14th St.
Tempe, AZ 85281

Matthew Gardiner
15 Waite Ct.
Providence, RI 02852

Martin Gardner
15 20th Ave.
Venice, CA 90291
310.306.6992

Blaise Gaston
686 Fairhope Ave.
Earlysville, VA 22936
434.973.1801
WWW.BLAISEGASTON.COM

Gareth Gaston
117 E 10th St. Apt 4
New York, NY 10003

Paul Gaston
810 Rugby Rd.
Charlottesville, VA 22903

Dayna Gedney
Sheridan College
Oakville, ON L6J7T8
Canada

Christopher Geisler
2863 Fall Creek Dr.
Grand Junction,
  CO 81503
970.523.9527

George Nakashima
  Woodworker, S.A
Mira Nakashima-Yarnall
1847 Aquetong Rd.
New Hope, PA 18938
215.862.2272
WWW.NAKASHIMAWOODWORKER.
  COM

Anton Gerner
24 Victoria Rd.
Hawthorn E
Victoria, VIC 3123
Australia
WWW.ANTONGERNER.COM.AU

David Getts
7 South Bellflower Rd.
Seattle, WA 98012
425.778.0110
WWW.DAVIDGETTSDESIGN.COM

David Geyer
9498 Smith Rd.
Waite Hill, OH 44094

Andrew Gieselman
18031 Panorama Dr.
Glencoe, MO 63038

Joanna Ginsberg
144 Milner Ave
Albany, NY 12208

Brian Gladwell
1801C Retallack St.
Regina, SK S4T 2J8
Canada

Andrew Glantz
Zenith Design
5450 E. Cortez Dr.
Scottsdale, AZ 85254
480.699.8803
WWW.ZENITH-DESIGN.COM

Andrew Glasgow
135 Lookout Dr.
Asheville, NC 28804

Andrew Glenn
39 N Bennet St. #3
Boston, MA 02113

Sophie Glenn
66 Ave. A, Apt. 5F
New York, NY 10009

Michael Gloor
51 Green St.
Peace Dale, RI 02879
401.782.2443

Kendall Glover
4858 S Evans Ave.
Chicago, IL 60615

Jenna Goldberg
75C Willow Street
Providence, RI 02909
JENNA@JENNAGOLDBERGSTUDIO.
    COM

Ronald Goldman
PO Box 452058
Los Angeles, CA 90045
310.216.9265

Miguel Gómez-Ibáñez
39 N Bennet St.
Boston, MA 02113
781.710.7007

Glendon Good
2945 Red Rock Loop Rd.
Sedona, AZ 86336-9194
928.282.6550

Taylor Goodale
206 Mill St.
Edinboro, PA 16412

Jordan Goodman,
    see JG Custom Design

John Stuart Gordon
309 Saint Ronan St.
New Haven, CT 06511

Hans Gottsacker
923 N 4th St. Apt 2
Marquette, MI 49855

Duncan Gowdy
45 South Rd.
Holden, MA 01520
508 829-8103
WWW.DUNCANGOWDY.COM

Michael Grace/
    David Fraser
Fine Woodworking Dept.
2001 Silver King Rd.
Nelson, BC V1L 1C8
Canada
250.352.6601, x286
WWW.SELKIRK.CA/PROGRAMS/
    TRADE

Marc Grainer
10615 Belfast Pl.
Potomac, MD 20854-1760
301.765.0649

Jason Gray
1118 Ann St.
Apt 7
Madison, WI 53713
WWW.JASONPETERGRAY.COM

David Greenwood
247 York St.
Jersey City, NJ 07302

Gregg Lipton
    Furniture, Inc.
Gregg Lipton
1 Mill Ridge Rd.
Cumberland, ME 04021
207.829.5010
WWW.LIPTONFURNITURE.COM

Grew-Sheridan Studio
John Sheridan
3450 Third St. #5-E
San Francisco, CA 94124
415.824.6161

David Grosz
53 Wildwood Rd.
Stamford, CT 06903
WWW.STUDIO2WOOD.COM

Josh Grove
4645 S Vandalia
Tulsa, OK 74135

Scott Grove
31 Riverview Drive
Rochester, NY 14623
SCOTT@SCOTTGROVE.COM

Glen Guarino
549 Pompton Ave.,
    Suite 125
Cedar Grove, NJ 07009
973.239.7867
WWW.GUARINOFURNITUREDESIGN.
    COM

Guenther Wood
    Group, Inc.
Greg Guenther
409 E York St.
Savannah, GA 31401
912.447.5522

Kino Guerin
276 Booth Rd.
Melbourne, QC J0B2B0
Canada

Nathalie Guez
522 Clarke
Montreal, QC H3Y 3C9
Canada

Adam Gunderson
3293 Valley Spring Rd.
Mt. Horeb, WI 53572

■:▋▋▋▋▋▋▋▋▋▋▋▋▋▋▋▋

H & J Bronze
    Sculpture Studio
Zhen Wu
498 Kennedy Blvd.
Bayonne, NJ 07002
973.214.0107
WWW.ZHENWUSCULPTURESTUDIO.
    COM

Coles Hairston
507 N Bluff Dr.
Austin, TX 78745

Half Crown - William Henry
Jodi Robbins
357 Huron Ave.
Cambridge, MA 02138

Mia Hall
1808 N Cleveland St.
Little Rock, AR 72207
501.683.7556

Charles Hamm
249 Maverick St. Apt. #7
Boston, MA 02128

Robin Hammer
713 White Oak Rd.
Charleston, WV 25302
304.344.8847

William Hammersley
1000 W Broad St.
Richmond, VA 23284-2522
804.828.4450

Ted Hammond
1035 E Olive St.
Bozeman, MT 59715
406.585.5556
WWW.HAMMONDWOODWORKING.
    COM

Peter Handler
3201 Fox St.
Philadelphia, PA 19129
215.225.0770
WWW.HANDLERSTUDIO.COM

Troy Hanson
7 W 34th St., Suite 1027
New York, NY 10001

Rob Hare
130 Carney Rd.
Ulster Park, NY 12487
845.658.3584

Alan Harp
4662 Christopher Ct.
Lilburn, GA 30047
WWW.ALANHARPDESIGN.COM

J. Michael Harrigan
9760 Indiana Pkwy.
Munster, IN 46321
WWW.ARCHACCENTS.COM

BA Harrington
420 Memphis Ave.
Madison, WI 53714
WWW.BAHARRINGTON.COM

Owain Harris,
    see O. H. Harris
    Cabinetmaker

Vincent Harris
4321 Pine Ave.
Erie, PA 16504

Peter Harrison
6280 Jockey St.
Middle Grove, NY 12850
WWW.LAVASSA.COM

Doug Haslam
1520 4th St. NW
Calgary, AB T2M 2Y9
Canada
403.230.0261

John Hassinen
1610 N Co Rd. 1200
Hamilton, IL 62341
608.289.3141

John Hatlestad
1830 N Rte. 83 Unit 1
Grayslake, IL 60030

Trautlinde Heater
PO Box V V
Aspen, CO 81612

Kyle Heffernan
5025 N. 68th St.
Scottsdale, AZ 85253
KYLEPHEFFERNAN@GMAIL.COM

Gary Hein
1 Asta Terrace
Santa Fe, NM 87508-8282

Roger Heitzman
750 Whispering Pines Dr.
Scotts Valley, CA 95066
831.461.1376
WWW.HEITZMANSTUDIOS.COM

Robb Helmkamp
88 Elk Mountain Rd.
Asheville, NC 28804
828.707.4863
WWW.KAMPSTUDIO.COM

Paul Henry,
    see Paul Henry Furniture

Bill Hergenroeder
10768 York Rd.
Cockeysville, MD 21030
410.666.5805

Christina Hilborne
#334 - 770 Fisgard St.
Victoria, BC V8W 0B8
Canada
WWW.SPLINTEREDMINX.COM

Jeffrey Hills
30 Rock Garden Gully
PO Box 1571
El Prado, NM 87529-1571

Robert Hitzig
154 Main St.
Montpelier, VT 05602
WWW.ROBERTHITZIG.COM

Ejler Hjorth-Westh
PO Box 73
Elk, CA 95432
707.877.3339

HMC
Vanessa Stappers
Arlandaweg 173-175
studycentre
Amsterdam, 1043 HR
Netherlands

James Hobza
1013 Tulip Way
Carlsbad, CA 92011

Stephen Hogbin
RR 2
Wiarton, ON N0H 2T0
Canada
519.534.5484

Holman Studios
Steve Holman
PO Box 572
171 Dogpatch Ln.
Dorset, VT 05251
802.867.0131

Roger Holmes
2124 Y St. Suite 109
Lincoln, NE 68503
402.570.0451

Holzman Custom Furniture
Pete Holzman
PO Box 882
54095 S Cir.
Idyllwild, CA 92549
WWW.NOBORINGFURNITURE.COM

Hyunsoo Hong
1875 Palmerston Ave.
West Vancouver, BC
V7V 2V3
Canada

Scott Hook
3218 32nd St.
San Diego, CA 92104
WWW.HOOKHANDMADE.COM

John and Robyn Horn
PO Box 17252
Little Rock, AR 72222-7252

Michael Hosaluk
RR# 2
Saskatoon, SK S7K 3J5
Canada
306.382.2380

John Houck
3654 Grand View Blvd.
Los Angeles, CA 90066
310.397.7993

Michael Hovey
8125 E Fairmount
Scottsdale, AZ 85251

Maren Hoye
3124 W Calhoun Blvd.
Apt. 405
Minneapolis, MN 55416

Hubel Handcrafted
Brian Hubel
1311 N Corona St.
Colorado Springs,
    CO 80903
719.667.0577
WWW.HUBELHI.COM

Thomas Hucker
49 Harrison Street
Hoboken,
    New Jersey 07030
WWW.THOMASHUCKERSTUDIO.COM

Katie Hudnall
604 Fine Arts Building
Murray, KY 42071
270.809.6748

Jeremy Hurn
485 Dorman Rd.
Bowen Island,
    BC V0N 1G1
Canada

David Hurwitz
23 Randolph Ave.
Randolph, VT 05060
802.728.9399
WWW.DAVIDHURWITZORIGINALS.
    COM

Erin Hutton
24 Mayfield St.
Portland, ME 04103-2520
207.749.4731

Matt Hutton
24 Mayfield St.
Portland, ME 04103-2520
207.749.4731

Stephen Hynson
PO Box 1110
Makawao, HI 96768
WWW.STEPHENHYNSON.COM

▬▬▬▬▬▬▬

Michael Iannone
162 W Lehigh Ave.
Philadelphia, PA 19133
WWW.IANNONEDESIGN.COM

Stephen Iino
202 W 107th St
New York, NY 10025
517.331.6835
NYIINO@YAHOO.COM
WWW.IINOINC.COM

Aren Irwin,
    see Artful Inventions

▬▬▬▬▬▬▬

Ann Rockler Jackson,
    see Rockler
    Woodworking
    & Hardware

Lili Jackson
4365 Willow Dr.
Medina, MN 55340
763.478.8201

James Rodenberger
    Master Woodworker
James Rodenberger
104 S 23rd St.
Terre Haute, IN 47803

Travis James
67 Metropolitan Ave.
Floor 2
Brooklyn, NY 11211

William E. Jewell
11064 Woodford Rd.
Woodford, VA 22580
WWW.HISTORICALWOODS.COM

JG Custom Design
Jordan Goodman
835 N. Wood St. #401
Chicago, IL 60622

John Thayer
  Cabinetmakers
John Thayer
Box 1670
62 Herring Creek Rd.
Vineyard Haven,
  MA 02568
508.627.0618
WWW.JOHNTHAYER.COM

Adrian Johnson
67 Mill Rd.
Fairhaven, MA 02719
WWW.FRIDGECOUCH.COM

Carl Johnson
1609 N Franklin St.
Tampa, FL 33602
813.494.5011

Craig Johnson
PO Box 131811
Saint Paul, MN 55113-0020
651.644.3652
STUDIOTUPLA.COM

Greg Johnson
216 Wadsworth Ave.
Avon, NY 14414
585.226.6730
WWW.JFRESTORATION.COM

Roger Johnson
141 Whitman Ave.
Whitman, MA 02382

Blaine Johnston
1513 Laurel Rd.
Wilkesboro, NC 28697

Robin Johnston
5846 Raven Rd.
Bloomfield Hills, MI 48301

Scott Johnston
6321 Tampa Ave.
Tarzana, CA 91335
818.708.3744
WWW.WOODEXTENSION.COM

Douglas Jones
433 Dennis Dr. NE
Los Lunas, NM 87031-8734
WWW.RANDOMORBITSTUDIO.COM

Sara Judy
3229 Jefferson Scio Dr.
PO Box 1010
Jefferson, OR 97352
800.238.8036
WWW.NWTIMBER.COM

K

Vladimir Kagan
1185 Park Ave. Apt. 14G
New York, NY 10128-1312

Danny Kamerath
5625 Mccommas Blvd.
Dallas, TX 75206
214.827.0674
WWW.DANNYKAMERATH.COM

Patrick Kana
6180 Waterloo Dr.
Easton, MD 21601

Mike Kaplan
401 S Wilson Blvd.
Nashville, TN 37205

Rita Kaplan
401 S Wilson Blvd.
Nashville, TN 37205

Peter Kasper
3411 IV Ave. SW
Tiffin, IA 52340

Stephen Keeble
4414 Walsh St.
Chevy Chase, MD 20815

Gordon Keller
10643 SW Riverside Dr.
Portland, OR 97219
415.238.8187

Clark Kellogg
2303-B Dunlavy
Houston, TX 77006
713.303.6256
WWW.KELLOGGFURNITURE.COM

Earl Kelly
7287 Shelby Ln.
Pensacola, FL 32526
850.944.0234
WWW.EARLKELLY.COM

John Kelsey
2148 Landis Valley Rd.
Lancaster, PA 17601
717.715.8630

Christopher Kemler
2729 Oak Trail
Carrollton, TX 75007

Stuart Kestenbaum
PO Box 518
Deer Isle, ME 04627-0518
207.348.2306
WWW.HAYSTACK-MTN.ORG

William Keyser, Jr.
8008 Taylor Rd.
Victor, NY 14564
585.742.2959

Shaun Killman
28 Lennon Pl.
Clifton, NJ 07013

George Kiorpelidis,
  see Missioncraft

John Kirschenbaum
664 154th Ave. NE
Bellevue, WA 98007
WWW.KBAUMDESIGN.COM

Meagan Klaassen
1217 Lyall St.
Victoria, BC V9A 5G8
Canada
250.380.1391

Charles Kline
340 Hammond St.
Chestnut Hill, MA 02467

Gerry Kmack
Cave Creek Woodworks
2000 Roush Dr.
Pagosa Springs, CO 81147

Susan Knox
476 Terrahue Rd.
Victoria, BC V9C 2B5
Canada

Charles Kolsky
1908 W Wyatt Earp Blvd.
Dodge City, KS 67801
620.227.5090

Kelly Komenda
825 S 49th St. Apt. 3
Philadelphia, PA 19143

Enrico Konig
975 Vernon Dr. Suite 250
Vancouver, BC V6A 3P2
Canada
604.255.0165

K.B. Koo
Sheridan College
Oakville, ON L6J7T8
Canada

Ken Koomalsingh
5471 S Ingleside Ave.
Apt. 2W
Chicago, IL 60615

Julie Koomler
1110 Linden St. Apt 1
Indianapolis, IN 46203

Sacha Kopachkov
Sheridan College
Oakville, ON L6J7T8
Canada

Silas Kopf
Silas Kopf
  Woodworking, Inc.
20 Stearns Ct.
Northampton, MA 01060
413.527.0284

Andrew Kopp
2 College St. #2446
Providence, RI 02903

Peter Korn
25 Mill St.
Rockport, ME 04856
207.594.5611

Mike Korsak
3505 Saxonburg Blvd.
Pittsburgh, PA 15238
WWW.MIKEKORSAK.COM

Sam Kragiel
1502 NW 6th St.
Gainesville, FL 32601
352.240.1414
WWW.BRAVESPACEDESIGN.COM

Joel Krakauer
623 15th St.
Bellingham, WA 98225

Justin Kramer
4981 Catoctin Dr.
  Apartment 46
San Diego, CA 92115

John Kriegshauser
3360 S State St.
Chicago, IL 60616
312.567.3259
CFDAINFO.ORG

Charles Krueger
526 Summit Ave.
Westfield, NJ 07090
908.251.4882

Amy Krupsky
5016 Baltan Rd.
Bethesda, MD 20816

Chris Kubash
12408 - 49 Ave NW
Edmonton, AB T6H 0H2
Canada
WWW.KUBASHSTUDIOFURNITURE.
    COM

Jacob Kulin
110 K Street
Boston, MA 02127
WWW.KULINMODERN.COM

Michael C. Kushlan
2512 Samaritan Ct.
Suite G
San Jose, CA 95124

Claiborne Kuzmich
4304 Molokai Dr.
Austin, TX 78749

Philip La Follette
5143 E Mann Rd
Pekin, IN 47165

Greg Laird
2841 S Grant St.
Englewood, CO 80113

Paul Lanante
1604-1360 White
   Oaks Blvd.
Oakville, ON L6H 2R7
Canada

Michael Landberg
PO Box 2278
Wolfeboro, NH 03894

Landers' Studio
Mark Landers
500 W St. Elmo Rd.
Austin, TX 78745
512.472.9663
WWW.LANDERSSTUDIO.COM

Laura Langford
Sheridan College
Oakville, ON L6J7T8
Canada

Mark Lanier
54 Welland Rd.
Brookline, MA 02445

Don Laporte
61 Charlrod Ave.
Somerset, MA 02726-4716
508.673.6074

Mark Laub,
    see Mark Laub Studios

Ian Laval
6844 Woodward Dr.
Brentwood Bay,
    BC V8M1A8
Canada
WWW.IANLAVAL.COM/WOOD/
    FURNITURE.

John Lavine
2434 9th St.
Berkeley, CA 94710
415.382.2865

Roch Laviolette
PO Box 358
5 Rideau St.
Westport, ON K0G 1X0
Canada

Daniel Lawrence
17 Quaker Rd.
Andover, NJ 07821
908.835.2807

Mark Leach
125 Burchard Hall
Blacksburg, VA 24061
540.231.5572

Todd Leback
1497 Dudley Mtn Rd.
Charlottesville, VA 22903

René LeBel
411 Canyon Close
Canmore, AB T1W 1H4
Canada

James Lee
3654 E Fall Crk. Pkwy. N Dr.
Indianapolis, IN 46205
317.924.9638

John Lee
1 Yonah Dr.
Atlanta, GA 30309-3320
404.444.9538

Jung-Eun Lee
121 John St., Thornhill
Toronto, ON L3T 1Y3
Canada

Kevin Leiby
435 Arlington Rd.
Redwood City, CA 94062

Alan Leland
6325 Kinard Rd.
Durham, NC 27703
919.596.5628

Po Shun Leong
8546 Oso Ave.
Winnetka, CA 91306
818.341.1559
WWW.POSHUNLEONG.COM

Peter Leue
19 Golder St.
Albany, NY 12209

Mark Levin
PO Box 94074
Albuquerque, NM 87199
505.490.9048
WWW.MARKLEVIN.COM

Aaron Levine
9954 NE Point View Dr.
Bainbridge Island,
    WA 98110
206.855.9101

Cody Lewis
311 Baltustrol Cir.
Roslyn, NY 11576

Dale Lewis
1372 Easley Bridge Rd.
Oneonta, AL 35121
WWW.DALEWIS.NET

Jeff Lewis
1631 Cantrell Blvd.
Conroe, TX 77301-4007
936.441.2470
WWW.JLEWISWOODCRAFT.COM

Scott Lewis
307 Gifford Dr.
Ennismore, ON K0L 1T0
Canada

Yoav Liberman
75W 119 St.
New York, NY 10026
WWW.YOAVLIBERMAN.COM

Tom Lie-Nielsen
PO Box 9
Warren, ME 04864

Scott Lincoln
428 Ada St.
Cincinnati, OH 45219

Bill Lindau
939 Vanderpool Rd.
Vilas, NC 28692
828.297.7566
WWW.LINDAUWOODWORKS.COM

Rex Lingwood
925924 Con. 13, RR#1
Bright, ON N0J 1B0
Canada
519.454.8263
WWW.MAKERSGALLERY.COM/
    REXLINGWOOD

Bruce Linthicum
Wallaby Woodworks
226 Whittlesey Road
Trenton, NJ 08618

Thomas Linville
7 Mount Pleasant Place
Rockport, MA 01966
TOM.LINVILLE@YAHOO.COM

Gregg Lipton,
    see Gregg Lipton
    Furniture, Inc.

Karla Little,
    see Fine
    Furnishings Shows

Michael Little
PO Box 904
Camden, ME 04843

Wayne Locke
9000 Feather Hill Rd.
Austin, TX 78737

Thomas Loeser
2826 Lakeland Ave.
Madison, WI 53704
608.262.9858

Roxanne Loncar
Sheridan College
Oakville, ON L6J7T8
Canada

Robin Long-Jordan
610 Rose Ln.
Mooresville, IN 46158

Ted Lott
1036 Williamson St. #3
Madison, WI 53703
WWW.TEDLOTT.COM/HOME.HTML

Victoria Lutz
Sheridan College
Oakville, ON L6J7T8
Canada

Kevin Lynch
2100 E Susquehanna Ave.
Philadelphia, PA 19125
WWW.TKLYNCHJOINERY.COM

Robert Lynch
3524 Williamsburg Ln. NW
Washington, DC 20008
202.371.2830

Martha Lynn
189 Upper Walden Rd.
Carmel, CA 93293
831.626.7166

M

Kern Maass
397 Rivers St.
Boone, NC 28608
828.262.6356

Kevin Mack
57 Madison St.
Malden, MA 02148
WWW.KEVINMACKFINEFURNITURE.
   COM

Tyler Mackenzie
10 Silvermoon Ave.
Bolton, ON L7E 2Y8
Canada

Rich Macrae
8 W Maple Rd.
Greenlawn, NY 11740

Gary Magakis
1129 N 3rd St.
Philadelphia, PA 19123

Jeremy Maher
1066-3 Linville Creek Rd.
Vilas, NC 28692

John Makepeace
Farrs, 3 Whitcombe Rd.
Beaminster Dorset
DT8 3NB
United Kingdom
+44.1308.862204

Merritt Malin
PO Box 7471
Boulder, CO 80306
303.775.4322
WWW.MERRITTMALIN.COM

Adam John Manley
111 Sheridan St. Apt 2
Portland, ME 04101
WWW.ADAMJOHNMANLEY.COM

Chris Mann
715 S 22nd St.
Arlington, VA 22202
703.629.8633
WWW.MANNDESIGNS.COM

Phillip Mann
1570 Garfield St.
Denver, CO 80206
WWW.PHILLIPMANNSTUDIOS.COM

Katy Mantyk
34 W 27th St. 5th Floor
New York, NY 10001
212.239.2808

Bill Manwiller
3319 65th Dr. NE
Marysville, WA 98270

John Marckworth
535 Cass St.
Port Townsend, WA 98368

Joel Mark
92 Rockledge Rd.
Hillsdale, NY 12529

Mark Del Guidice
   Furniture Maker
Mark Del Guidice
61 Endicott St., Bld. # 32
Norwood, MA 02062
781.769.6333
WWW.MARKDELGUIDICE.COM

Mark Laub Studios
Mark Laub
3750 211th Ln. NW
Oak Grove, MN 55303
763.753.1368

Amy Markanda
770 Othello St.
Mississauga, ON L5W 1Y3
Canada

Michael Markland
10966 Oxbow Dr.
Komoka, ON N0L 1R0
Canada

David Marks
2128 Marsh Rd.
Santa Rosa, CA 95403
707.526.2763

Kyle Marlin
200 Ranchcrest Rd.
Lorenz, TX 76655
254.751.2200

Gay Marshall
32 Wistar Rd.
Paoli, PA 19301

Kerry Marshall
10951 Gurley Ln.
Mendocino, CA 95460
707.937.5051
WWW.MENDOCINOFURNITURE.COM/
   ARTIST

Alastair Martin
5 Beechwood Ln.
St. Clements, ON N0B 2M0
Canada

Brian Martin
110 Edith Margaret Pl.
Arnprior, ON K2W 1A8
Canada

Brigitte Martin
461 Cochran Rd.
PO Box 103
Pittsburgh, PA 15228
WWW.CRAFTHAUS.NING.COM

Chris Martin
1512 Florida Ave.
Ames, IA 50014

Loy Martin
150 Grant Ave. #F
Palo Alto, CA 94306
650.325.3416
WWW.LOYMARTINFURNITURE.COM

Wendy Maruyama
4565 Alice St.
San Diego, CA 92115
619.594.6511

Sherry Masters
Grovewood Gallery
111 Grovewood Rd.
Asheville, NC 28804
WWW.GROVEWOOD.COM

Blase Mathern, Jr.
3563 Polk Cir. E
Wellington, CO 80549
WWW.BLASEMATHERNJR.COM

Michael Mau
122 Poplar Ct.
Neenah, WI 54956
WWW.MAUHAUS.COM

Laura Mays
258 Shelburne Line Rd.
Colrain, MA 01340

Austin McAdams
401 W Marshall St.
Richmond, VA 23220

John McAlevey
364 Four Rod Rd.
Warren, ME 04864

Karen McBride
3133 Woodkilton Rd.
Dunrobin, ON K0A 1T0
Canada
613.832.8071
WWW.WOODKILTONSTUDIO.COM

Tim McCarthy
5086 Nighthawk Way
San Diego, CA 92056

Al McClain,
   see Al McClain
   Woodworking

Paul McClelland
11135 SW 78th Ct.
Miami, FL 33156

Jason McCloskey
42 E Transit St. #2
Providence, 02906

Sarah McCollum
PO Box 1421
El Prado, NM 87529
505.770.2699

Michael McCoy
97 Castle Dr.
Groton, MA 01450

Steve McDonald
10 Hunter Dr.
Hughesville, PA 17756

Robert McDonald
220 N Dithridge St.
Apt 405
Pittsburgh, PA 15213

Michael McDunn
741 Rutherford Rd.
Greenville, SC 29609
864.242.0311
WWW.MCDUNNSTUDIO.COM

Tom McFadden
PO Box 162
Philo, CA 95415
WWW.MCFADDENFURNITURE.COM

Keith McIntosh
PO Box 55
Chatham, MA 02633
617.650.8221
WWW.KWMCINTOSH.COM

Judy McKie
82 Holworthy St.
Cambridge, MA 02138
781.391.2333

Dale McLoud
269 Meadow Ln.
Murfreesboro, TN 37128

Tina McLuckie
3 Salem St.
Portland, ME 04102

Tom McMillan
38 Terrapin Trail
Whittier, NC 28789
828.497.0060

Andrew McSheffrey
151 Gilmanton Rd.
Belmont, NH 03220
603.608.7427

Gordon Meacham II
2647 Garfield St.
San Mateo, CA 94403
650.222.9415

Mechthild Wagner,
    see Art Beyond Borders

Sharon Mehrman
28 Harold St.
Florence, MA 01062

James Mellick
15040 Maple Ridge Rd.
Milford Center, OH 43045
937.349.8408

William Melton
1830 Lone Eagle Ct.
Reno, NV 89521

Walt Mertz,
    see Vision Furniture
    Design

Ryan Messier
1670 State Rd.
Plymouth, MA 02360

Mario Messina
148 Main Street
Cambridge, VT 05444

Naomi Mest
148 Myrtle Ct.
Arcata, CA 95521

Derrick Method
608 W Walnut St.
Nappanee, IN 46550
WWW.DERRICKMETHODDESIGNS.
    COM

Jesse Meyer,
    see Pergamena
    Handmade Parchments,
    Artisanal Leathers and
    Applied Arts

Gregg Mich,
    see Dapwood Furniture

Karl Mielke
6000 Randolph St.
Lincoln, NE 68510

Aaron Miley
7165 American Way
Apt. G
Indianapolis, IN 46256

Rob Millard-Mendez
1721 Bayard Park Dr.
Evansville, IN 47714

Dennis Miller
200 Lexington Ave.
Suite 1210
New York, NY 10016

Claudia Mills
3823 Pearl St.
Philadelphia, PA 19104
215.386.2347
WWW.CLAUDIAMILLS.COM

Missioncraft
George Kiorpelidis
110 Rue Cedarcrest
Dollard-Des-Ormeaux,
    QC H9A 1G3
Canada

Charles Mitchell
5042 Scotts Valley Dr.
Suite A
Scotts Valley, CA 95066

James Mitlyng
2955 Fillmore St. NE
Minneapolis, MN 55418

Moderne Gallery
Robert Aibel
111 N 3rd. St.
Philadelphia, PA 19106
215.740.4875

Hugh Montgomery
14645 Sunrise Dr. NE
Bainbridge Island,
    WA 98110
360.779.8300
WWW.HUGHMONTGOMERY.COM

Jamie Moon
Sheridan College
Oakville, ON L6J7T8
Canada

Lois Moran
400 Central Park W #20K
New York, NY 10025
212.274.0630

Julie Morringello
26 School St.
Stonington, ME 04681
207.367.0958

Benjamin Morris
40 Huntersfield Rd.
Delmar, NY 12054

Pat Morrow
420 Snyder Mountain Rd.
Evergreen, CO 80439
303.674.1203
WWW.TRAILMIXSTUDIO.COM

Laura Mosena
1610 N Co Rd. 1200
Hamilton, IL 62341
608.289.3141
WWW.HMWOODWORKS.COM

C. Merrill Motor
550 S 4th St.
Louisville, KY 40202

Jim Motto
321 Belt Ave. Unit# 401
St. Louis, MO 63112

Sabiha Mujtaba
1078 Deleon Dr.
Clarkston, GA 30021-0127
404.228.1010

Joseph Murphy
717 Spruce St.
Madison, WI 53715
608.556.5970
WWW.JOSEPHMURPHY.NET

Mira Nakashima-Yarnal,
    see George Nakashima
    Woodworker, S.A

Kevin Nathanson
3705 High Meadow Rd.
Chapel Hill, NC 27514

Eric Nation
117 E Louisa St.
PMB 135
Seattle, WA 98102
808.205.8351

Lloyd Natoff
1217 W Monroe
Chicago, IL 60607
312.733.4205
WWW.SINATOF.COM

Matthew Nauman
5595 Rivendell Pl.
Frederick, MD 21703
570.295.0777

Nelson Designs, LLC
Craig Nelson
149 Whalehead Rd.
Gales Ferry, CT 06335

Brad Nelson
209A, AABC
Aspen, CO 81611
970.309.3493

Dale Nelson Jr.
PO Box 201
119 Lindsay Tr.
Edwards, CO 81632
WWW.PARAGONWOODWORKING.
    COM

Dan Neubauer
157 University Vlg. Unit E
Ames, IA 50010

Brian Newell
1005 Cedar St.
Ft. Bragg, CA 95437
WWW.BRIANNEWELLFURNITURE.COM

Richard Newman
89 Canal St.
Rochester, NY 14608
585.328.1577

Bart Niswonger
481 Kinne Brook Rd.
Worthington, MA 01098
413-320-5930
WWW.BARTNISWONGER.COM

Tim Nuanes
1108 Kingston Lane
Ventura, CA 93001
WWW.TIMNUANES.COM

Craig Nutt
1307 Kingston Springs Rd.
Kingston Springs, TN 37082
615.952.4308
WWW.CRAIGNUTT.COM

O. H. Harris Cabinetmaker
Owain Harris
63 Nottingham Rd.
Deerfield, NH 03037
WWW.HARRISCABINETMAKER.COM

Daniel Oates,
  see dbO Home

Francis O'Brien
411 Walnut St.
Harrisburg, PA 17101

Terry O'Donnell
323 Vincent Dr.
Mountain View,
  CA 94041-2211
408.536.6693

Richard Oedel
86 Marlborough St. #3
Boston, MA 02116
617.763.1349

William O'Kane
PO Box 385
35 King St. East
Colborne, ON K0K 1S0
Canada
WWW.ORIJINSTUDIO.COM

James Oleson
1421 Gray Bluff Tr.
Chapel Hill, NC 27517
919.968.3659

Michael Oleson
Rua Vale Do Santo
  Antonio 6, 3
Lisboa, 1170-380
Portugal
351.96.946.6478
WWW.MIKEOLESON.COM

Faithe Olson
3960 Grand River Ave.
Apt 3
Detroit, MI 48208

Jere Osgood
626 Abbot Hill Rd.
Wilton, NH 03086-9129
603.654.2960

Todd Ouwehand
12014 Mitchell Ave.
Los Angeles, CA 90066
310.903.9257

Allan Parachini
1088 N Holliston Ave.
Pasadena, CA 91104
626.676.5328
WWW.CUSTOMMADE.COM

Cynthia Park
143 Beverly Rd.
Asheville, NC 28805
828.296.0851

Todd Partridge
PO Box 7101
San Diego, CA 92167

Timothy Pastore
379 Albion St.
Wakefield, MA 01880

Jill Patrick
409 Kingston Cres.
Winnipeg, MB R2M 0T7
Canada

Lance Patterson
31 Queensberry St. #4
Boston, MA 02215

Paul Henry Furniture
Paul Henry
2633 State St.
Carlsbad, CA 92008
760.434.4270
WWW.PAULHENRYFURNITURE.COM

Chris Pearsell-Ross
Sheridan College
Oakville, ON L6J7T8
Canada

Richard Peirce, Jr.
158 Greenmeadow Dr.
Timonium, MD 21093

Andrew Peklo, III
29 Pomperaug Rd.
Woodbury, CT 06798
203.263.4566
WWW.PEKLODESIGNANDJOINERY.
  COM

Jay Penner
210 Arch Hall
Lincoln, NE 68588-0106

Pergamena
  Handmade Parchments,
  Artisanal Leathers
  and Applied Arts
Jesse Meyer
11 Factory St.
Montgomery, NY 12549

Kyle Peters
Sheridan College
Oakville, ON L6J7T8
Canada

David Petersen
10203 Oak Hollow Dr.
Austin, TX 78758-5534
512.836.5275

Larry Peterson
11000 E Pleasant Pl.
Gold Canyon, AZ 85118
480.671.8494

Myrl Phelps Jr.
76 Ragged Mountain Rd.
Danbury, NH 03230

Timothy Philbrick
PO Box 555
218 Ocean Rd.
Narragansett, RI 02882
401.789.4030

Michael Pietragalla
88 Hatch St., Loft 406
New Bedford, MA 02745
508.997.1079

Kurt Piper
PO Box 51502
Indian Orchard, ME 01151
WWW.PIPERWOODWORKING.COM

Norman Pirollo
8226 Rodney Farm Dr.
Ottawa, ON K0A 2P0
Canada
613.821.5160
WWW.REFINEDEDGE.COM

Piscataqua Design, LLC
Matt Wajda
PO Box 580
Rollinsford, NH 03801

Andrew Pitts
667 Courthouse Rd.
Heathsville, VA 22473
804.724.3401
WWW.ANDREWPITTSFURNITUREMAKER.
  COM

Daniel Pittsford
PO Box 75144
Seattle, WA 98175
206.255.7377

Christopher Poehlmann
C. Poehlmann Studio, Inc.
3201 Fox St.
Philadelphia, PA 19129
866.597.4800
WWW.CPLIGHTING.COM

George Poelker
405 W 3rd Ave.
Windermere, FL 34786

Dan Pohl
9654 Krogwold Rd.
Amjerst Jct, WI 54407

Margaret Polcawich
7508 Nutwood Ct.
Derwood, MD 20855-2232
301.990.9070
WWW.HANDSCULPTEDFURNITURE.
  COM

Donna Popke
PO Box 483
Suttons Bay, MI 49682
231.271.6950

Alice Porembski
2579 Russell St.
Redding, CA 96001
530.243.6132

Earl Powell
44 Brookside Ave.
Winchester, MA 01890

Tim Preece
5065 Cook Rd.
Ashville, OH 43103

Richard Prisco
892 Windwood Ln.
Boone, NC 28607
912.660.2376

Elaine Proll
35 Ross Rd.
Livingston, NJ 07039

Dean Pulver
PO Box 1457
El Prado, NM 87529-1457
505.751.4402
WWW.DEANPULVER.COM

Michael Puryear
46 Longyear Rd.
Shokan, NY 12481
845.943.5975
WWW.MICHAELPURYEAR.COM

R S Design Group
Matt Snyder
282 Joes Hill Rd.
Brewster, NY 10509
484.239.5758
WWW.RSDESIGNGROUP.COM

Charles Radtke
W62 N732 Riveredge Dr.
Cedarburg, WI 53012

Mike Randall
1417 Pembroke St.
Victoria, BC V8R 1V7
Canada

David Rasmussen
345 Colorado Ave.
Suite 207
Carbondale, CO 81623
970.963.6689
WWW.DAVIDRASMUSSENDESIGN.
    COM

Martin Ratermann
PO Box 100
Rocheport, MO 65279
573.698.2192

Jon Rawlinson
1835 Mackinnon Ave.
Cardiff, CA 92007

Andrew Redington
University Of Wisconsin
Oshkosh-Art Dept.
800 Algoma Blvd.
Oshkosh, WI 54901

Lauren Reed
Sheridan College
Oakville, ON L6J7T8
Canada

James Reedy
22346 Treetop Cir.
Boca Raton, FL 33433

Brian Reid
40 Warren
Rockland, ME 04841
BRIAN@BRIANREIDFURNITURE.COM
WWW.BRIANREIDFURNITURE.COM

John Reilly
611 Devonshire St.
Pittsburgh, PA 15213

Roy Rejean
271 des Vosges
St-Lambert, Quebec
J4S 1M1
Canada

Clark Renfort
PO Box 567
Laytonville, CA 95454

Susan Rennie
2046 48th Ave.
San Francisco, CA 94116

Scott Reuman
7425 Magnolia Dr.
Nederland, CO 80466
WWW.CONUNDRUMDESIGNS.COM

Reznikoff Custom
    Furniture, Inc.
Michael Reznikoff
328 Thomas Pl.
Everman, TX 76140
817.478.2731

Rhode Island School of
    Design, Furniture Design
2 College St.
Providence, RI 02903
WWW.RISD.EDU/FURNITURE.CF

Susan Ricca
154 Old Newtown Rd.
Monroe, CT 06468-1106
203.459.4414

Richard Frinier Collection
Richard Frinier
4324 E Broadway
Long Beach, CA 90803
WWW.RICHARDFRINIER.COM

Austin Richards
130 Village Dr.
Boone, NC 28607
WWW.FACEBOOK.COM/
    AUSTINRICHARDSF

David Richardson
24 Logan St. N 521
New Bedford, MA 02740
508.676.1760
WWW.NESTUDIOFURNITURE.COM

Marc Richardson
7175 Marconi
Montreal, QC H2S 3K4
Canada
514.934.3960
WWW.MRDESIGNS.CA

Robert Rickard
PO Box 1360
Taos, NM 87571
WWW.RICKARDSTUDIO.COM

Ray Riddell
117 Eastview Dr.
Coventry, CT 06238
860.742.0254
WWW.WHITEDOVEWOODWORKING.
    COM

Chris Rifkin
12 Causeway Rd.
Hingham, MA 02043
781.749.4013

Cheryl R. Riley
150 Bay St. #824
Jersey City, NJ 07302
201.362.3174

Samuel Rivett
6290 Starfield Cres.
Mississauga, ON L5N 1X4
Canada

Jodi Robbins,
    see Half Crown
    - William Henry

Mike Robbins
2200 Bull Run Dr.
Apex, NC 27539
919.779.0719

Robert Erickson
    Woodworking
Robert Erickson
18977 Wepa Way
Nevada City, CA 95959
530.292.3777
WWW.ERICKSONWOODWORKING.
    COM

Cory Robinson
4148 Vera Dr.
Indianapolis,
    IN 46220-5295
317.205.9072

Dennis Rocheleau
460 Papurah Rd.
Fairfield, CT 06825

Rockler Woodworking
    & Hardware
Ann Rockler Jackson
4365 Willow Dr.
Medina, MN 55340-9701
763.478.8216

Richard Rode
2521 Schell Ct. NE
Albuquerque, NM 87106
505.266.6384

Kevin Rodel
13 Lincoln St.
Brunswick, ME 04011
207.725.7252
WWW.KEVINRODEL.COM

James Rodenberger,
    see James Rodenberger
    Master Woodworker

Jack Rodie
4 Deacon Dr.
York, ME 03909
207.451.2130
WWW.JACKRODIE.COM

Tom Rojcik
Sheridan College
Oakville, ON L6J7T8
Canada

Seth Rolland
1039 Jackson St.
Port Towsend, WA 98368
360.379.0414
WWW.SETHROLLAND.COM

Gabriel Romeu
315 Crosswicks-
    Ellisdale Rd.
Chesterfield, NJ 08515
609.291.8624
WWW.STUDIOFURNITURE.COM

Jim Rose
8693 County Rd. D
Forestville, WI 54213-9626
920.825.7422

Nathan Rose
6325 W Wilkinson Blvd.
Suite D
Belmont, NC 28012
704.829.5059
WWW.NATHANROSEFURNITURE.COM

Roskear Fine Furniture
Timothy Ellsworth
PO Box 515
116 E. Weatogue St.
Simsbury, CT 06070
860.651.9526

Edward Ross
1401 Presque Isle Ave.
Marquette, MI 49855

Rejean Roy
271 Des Vosges
St-Lambert, QC J4S 1M1
Canada
450.923.0103

Richard Ruminski
Sheridan College
Oakville, ON L6J7T8
Canada

Thomas Russell
76 Franklin St.
Braintree, MA 02184

Jennifer Rust
2130 Grand Ave. Apt. #4
San Diego, CA 92109

Patricia Ryan
353 Park St.
West Roxbury, MA 02132

Vincent Ryan
745 Atlantic Ave. 11th Fl.
Boston, MA 02111
617.357.9031

Mitch Ryerson
Ryerson Designs
12 Upton St.
Cambridge, MA 02139
781.391.1231

S

James Sagui
820 25th St. #4
West Palm Beach, FL
   33407
561.833.0252
WWW.JAMESBSAGUI.COM

Mike Salguero
99 First St.
Cambridge, MA 04864

Arne Salonen
PO Box 192732
San Francisco, CA 94119
415.596.4695

Carol Salvin
6612 Gunn Dr.
Oakland, CA 94611

Sam Maloof
   Woodworker, Inc.
Roslyn Bock
PO Box 8051
5131 Carnelian St.
Alta Loma, CA 91701

Franky Sanche
Sheridan College
Oakville, ON L6J7T8
Canada

Lary Sanders
804 Riverside Dr.
Springfield, OH 45504
937.399.4126
WWW.LARYSANDERS.COM

Peter Sandoval
5311 Joe Wilson Rd.
Midlothian, TX 76065
469.766.1069

Albert Santoni
1412 Walker St.
Iron Mountain, MI 49801
906.774.5800

Jeffrey Scanlan
4733 Banks St.
New Orleans, LA 70119

Roy Schack
PO Box 886
Spring Hill, QLD 4004
Australia
+61.4.1532.8166
WWW.ROYSCHACK.COM

Peter Schlebecker
3922 Kincaid Terrace
Kensington, MD 20895
301.377.9825
WWW.SCHLEBECKERSTUDIOS.COM

Steve Schmiedl
1927 W Greenleaf Ave.
Chicago, IL 60626
773.338.6516

Jason Schneider
PO Box 5598
Snowmass Village,
   CO 81615
858.922.7002

Andres Schneiter
24705-108 Ave.
Maple Ridge, BC
V2W 1G7
Canada
604.467.2287

The School at
   Annapolis Woodworks
Troy Beall
3312 Rodeo Dr.
Davidsonville, MD 21035

Libby Schrum
5 Harden Ave.
Camden, ME 04843
WWW.LIBBYSCHRUM.COM

Schuettinger Conservation
   Services, Inc.
Bruce Schuettinger
PO Box 244
17 N Alley
New Market, MD 21774
301.865.3009

Andrew Schultz
4021 S 35th St.
Lincoln, NE 68506

Paul Schurch
Schürch Woodwork
731 Bond Ave.
Santa Barbara, CA 93103
805-965-3821
WWW.SCHURCHWOODWORK.COM

Richard Scobey
257 E Groverdale St.
Covina, CA 91722
626.695.8144

Frances (Shelley) Scott
814 W Mulberry Apt B
Denton, TX 76201
WWW.SHELLEYSCOTTSTUDIO.COM

Jay Scott
1711 5th Ave. SE
Olympia, WA 98501
360.456.8799

Kelly Scott
3716 Canon Gate Cir.
Carrollton, TX 75007

Maxx Scroter
Sheridan College
Oakville, ON L6J7T8
Canada

Adrien Segal
1007 A Guerrero St.
San Francisco, CA 94110
303.908.4690

Scott Severns
59 Far View Rd.
Great Meadows, NJ 07838

Wyatt Severs
905 Olive St.
Murray, KY 42071

Steve Shafer
4140 Howard Ave.
Kensington, MD 20895

Harold Shapiro
5454 Yohe Rd.
Waynesboro, PA 17268
717.352.3001

Michele Sommer-Shapiro
5454 Yohe Rd.
Waynesboro, PA 17268
717.352.3001
WWW.SDESIGNG.COM

Chuck Sharbaugh
14039 Candlewick Dr.
Holly, MI 48442-9505

Alf Sharp
3130 Doolittle Rd.
Woodbury, TN 37190
615.563.2831
WWW.ALFREDSHARP.COM

Chris Shea
4700 Danville Rd.
Brandywine, MD 20613
WWW.CHRISSHEA.COM

Christine Shenkman
3739 Aberdeen Way
Houston, TX 77025
WWW.ARTBETWEENSPACES.COM

John Sheridan,
   see Grew-
   Sheridan Studio

Tom Shields
81 Annandale Ave.
Asheville, NC 28801

Matthew Shively,
   see Cerca Trova Design

Lynn Shoger
1874 Andrew Pl.
Paradise, CA 95969

Don Shomaker
1834 Cambridge Ave.
College Park, GA 30337
WWW.OUTYONDER.NET

David Short
73 W Shore Dr.
Pennington, NJ 08534

Robert Simons
127 Conway St.
Carlisle, PA 17013
717.254.6434

Martin Simpson
59 Mabel St.
Portland, ME 04103

Tommy Simpson
PO Box 2264
New Preston, CT 06777
860.868.0021

Michael Singer
1170 El Solyo Heights Dr.
Felton, CA 95018
831.335.3167
WWW.MSFINEWOODWORKING.COM

Carter Sio
1690 Newtown-
   Langhorne Rd.
Newtown, PA 18940
215.962.7923
WWW.CARTERJASONSIO.COM

Theodore Slavin
228 Corliss Ave.
Johnson City, NY 13790
607.729.8206
WWW.SLAVINSWORKBENCH.COM

Lee Smeltz
146 Radcliff Terrace
Souderton, PA 18964
215.723.0318

Brad Smith,
   see Bradford
   Woodworking

Isabel Smith-Stuart
Sheridan College
Oakville, ON L6J7T8
Canada

Janice Smith
715 S 7th St.
Philadelphia, PA 19147
215.923.1447
WWW.JANICESMITHFURNITURE.COM

Jonathan Smith
359 Ft. Washington Ave.
   Suite 1G
New York, NY 10033

Lance Smith
310 56th Ave
Greeley, CO 80634

Paul Smith
1349 Lexington Ave.
New York, NY 10128

Scott Smith
310 Jefferson Dr.
Pittsburgh, PA 15228
412.268.2291

Warren Snow
9674 Ridge View Dr.
Marshall, VA 20115
WWW.SNOWWOODWORKS.COM

Matt Snyder,
   see R S Design Group

Christopher Solar
30 Euclid Ave.
Ottawa, ON K1S 2W3
Canada
613.730.0540
WWW.CHRISTOPHERSOLAR.COM

Jacob Sorenson
955 Hulsey Ct. SE
Salem, OR 97302

Sorraia Studios
Clinton (Clint) Struthers
304 W Wackerly St.
Suite A100
Midland, MI 48640
989.750.2453
WWW.SORRAIASTUDIOS.COM

Jerry Spady
108 E Geneva Lane
Oak Ridge, TN 37830
865-483-1228

Fred Spencer
2105 Constance Dr.
Oakville, ON L6J 5V1
Canada
905.845.0217

Dolly Spragins
Chicago, IL
773.752.7267
WWW.DOLLYSPRAGINS.COM

Patricia Spragins
1166 E 53rd St
Chicago, IL 60615

Worth Squire
PO Box 248
College Grove, TN 37046
615.368.7798

Shane Staley
1046 N. Honore St. Apt. 2R
Chicago, IL 60622

Frank Stanek
33640 Ashley Pl. PO Box 98
Greenfield, CA 93927
831.674.0119

Jay Stanger
P.O. Box 494
South Easton, MA 02375
WWW.JAYSTANGER.COM

Nicholas Stawinski
353 Highland
Rochester, MI 48307

Joe Stearns
6941 N Long Lake Rd.
Traverse City, MI 49684
231.995.9427
WWW.JOESTEARNSFURNITURE.COM

Steckley Designs, Inc.
Mr. Matthew Steckley
15832 118 Terrace N
Jupiter, FL 33478
WWW.STECKLEY.COM

John Stephens
1607 Salvador Pl.
Santa Fe, NM 87501

Michael Sterling
PO Box 4374
Chico, CA 95927

Charles Sthreshley
402 Duncan St.
Ashland, VA 23005-1908
202.639.1797
WWW.CONCRETE-ART.COM

David Stine
16376 Bartlett Rd.
Dow, IL 62022-3030
WWW.STINEWOODWORKING.COM

Allen Stone
411 W Republican St. #107
Seattle, WA 98119

Doug Stowe
PO Box 247
Eureka Springs, AR 72632
479.253.7387

David Strauss
14 Grayson Ln.
Newton, MA 02462
617.527.0010

Aaron Stubbs
2454 Lofton Rd. SW
Roanoke, VA 24015
WWW.ACORNFABRICATION.COM

Andrea Summerton
181 Monitor St.
Brooklyn, NY 11222
WWW.ALSDESIGNS.COM

Alison Swann-Ingram
1609 N Franklin St.
Tampa, FL 33602
813.503.7061

Lynn Szymanski
PO Box 315
Rollinsford, NH 03869

John Tagiuri
John Tagiuri Studios'
Somerville, MA 02145
WWW.JTSCULPTURESTUDIOS.COM

Tangram Woodworks
Terry Bachman
424 Virginia Ave.
Cumberland, MD 21502
301.633.2389

Rich Tannen
585 HF Five Points Road
Honeoye Falls, NY 14472
WWW.RICHTANNEN.COM

Charlie Tanner
Sheridan College
Oakville, ON L6J7T8
Canada

Robert Taormina
5400 Gullen Mall -
   Art Bldg. Rm 150
Wayne State University
Detroit, MI 48202
313.577.2980
WWW.ART.WAYNE.EDU

Matthew Teague
3613 Brush Hill Ct.
Nashville, TN 37216
615.258.3633
WWW.MATTHEWTEAGUE.COM

Scott Temple
38 Griego Hill Rd.
Tesuque, NM 87504

Phillip Tennant
5116 Knollton Rd.
Indianapolis, IN 46228
317.253.9307

Brian Tepfenhart
48 Norfolk St. Apt. 3
Cambridge, MA 02139

Abraham Tesser
308 W Lake Dr.
Athens, GA 30606
706.543.4332
WWW.TESSERFURNITURE.COM

John Thayer,
    see John Thayer
    Cabinetmakers

Diane Thede
413 E Lima Ave.
Ada, OH 45810
419.634.6290

Les Thede
413 E Lima Ave.
Ada, OH 45810
419.634.6290
WWW.EVERLASTINGFURNITURE.COM

Robert Then
25 Greenfield St.
Buffalo, NY 14214-1914
716.832.8707

Don Thomas
45 Lispenard St.
New York, NY 10013
212.925.6868

James Thomas
PO Box 957
Niwot, CO 80544

John Thomas
107 Lanier Ln.
Mauldin, SC 29662
864.915.7797
WWW.THEJOINERYGALLERY.COM

William Thomas
15 Todd Hill Road
Rindge, NH 03461
603-899-3249
WWW.WILLIAMTHOMAS-FURNITURE.
    COM

Matt Thomson
3449 Brennan Line
Orillia, ON L3V 6H3
Canada

Thomas Throop
26 Grove St.
New Canaan, CT 06840
203.966.5798
WWW.BLACKCREEKDESIGNS.COM

William Thuburn
87 Rue Des Atrebates
Brussels, 1040
Belgium

Robert Tiffany
27 Cafferty Rd.
Point Pleasant, PA 18950

Charles Todd
7054 Germantown Ave.
Philadelphia, PA 19119
215.248.4391
WWW.TODDFURNITURE.COM

Joshua Torbick
252 Wibird St.
Portsmouth, NH 03801

Allen Townsend
12 Durham Dr.
Andover, MA 01810-5500
978.475.9575

Richard Townsend
243 Increase Miller Rd.
Katonah, NY 10536
914.232.5867
WWW.RICHARDMAKESFURNITURE.
    COM

Albert Trapuzzano
44 Laurel Dr.
Holtwood, PA 17532
717.284.5143

Nancy Trapuzzano
44 Laurel Dr.
Holtwood, PA 17532
717.284.5143

Joe Trippi
43737 Dorisa Ct.
Northville, MI 48167
DEBBEESHEPPARD.COM

Heather Trosdahl
428 N Harrison St. Apt. A
Fort Bragg, CA 95437

Paul Troyano
4738 Palmyra St.
New Orleans, LA 70119

Michael Tudor
2041 Anna Dr.
Elkhart, IN 46514-3126
574.264.6078

Bud Tullis
PO Box 434
Solvang, CA 93464
805.688.3758

Kristin Turner
133 Spring Valley Rd.
Westerville, OH 43081

Peter Turner
126 Boothby Ave.
South Portland, ME 04106
207.799.5503
WWW.PETERSTURNER.COM

Carl Twarog
PO Box 33
Fountain, NC 27829-0033

Joseph Twichell
66 Prospect St.
Pawcatuck, CT 06379
860.599.1248

Devin Tyman
51 Chamberlain St
Holliston, MA 01746

▬▬▮▬▬▬▬▬▬

Joël Urruty
801 19th St. SW
Hickory, NC 28602
828.304.1224
WWW.JOELURRUTY.COM

◢▬▬V▬▬▬▬▬

Scott Van Cleef
3287 Springwood Rd.
Fincastle, VA 24090
540.473.8681

Nakisha VanderHoeven,
    see Fine Wood Artists /
    Nakisha.com

Chris Vanderwal
Sheridan College
Oakville, ON L6J7T8
Canada

Anthony Jay Van Dunk,
    see Anthony Van Dunk:
    Woodworker

Dylan Vankleef
40 Cross St. RR 1
Enterprise, ON K0K 1Z0
Canada

Michael VanOverbeck
4633 Marine Ave. #211
Lawndale, CA 90260

Andy Vasquez
1550 Fourth St.
Bethlehem, PA 18020

Bob Vergette
1103 Walden Rd. RR 1
Pender Island, BC
V0N 2M1
Canada
250.629.3820

Kerry Vesper
116 E Ellis Dr.
Tempe, AZ 85282
480.429.0954
WWW.KERRYVESPER.COM

J-P Vilkman
15 Shepley Street H
Portland, ME 04101
WWW.J-PVILKMAN.COM

Vision Furniture Design
Walt Mertz
12444 Popes Head Rd.
Clifton, VA 20124

John Vlah
3042 Holley Rd.
Glen Rock, PA 17327

◢▬▬W▬▬▬▬▬

Robin Wade
803 Hermitage Dr.
PMB 4124
Florence, AL 35630

Matt Wajda, see
    Piscataqua Design, LLC

Karen Wales
24 Long Cove Point Rd.
Chamberlain, ME 04541

Bilhenry Walker
4038 N 6th St.
Milwaukee, WI 53212
414.698.1171
WWW.BILHENRYGALLERY.COM

Andrew Wallace
122-C E Fir St.
Fort Bragg, CA 95437

A. Thomas Walsh
PO Box 482
West Stockbridge,
   MA 01266-0482
413.232.0249
WWW.ATHOMASWALSH.COM

Brendan Walsh
1571 Cleveland Rd. Apt. 2
Bogart, GA 30622
WWW.BRENDANWALSH-
   STUDIOFURNITURE.COM

Seth Walter
63 Beechwood Ln.
South Windsor, CT 06074
860.796.7204
WWW.SILVERLEAFWOODWORKING.
   COM

Paulus Wanrooij
708 Harpswell Neck Rd.
Harpswell, ME 04079
207.833.5026
WWW.PAULUSFURNITURE.COM

Andrew Ward
908 Porphyry St.
P.O. Box 693
Ophir, CO 81426

Geoffrey Warner
43 N Main St.
PO Box 710
Stonington, ME 04681
207.367.6555
WWW.GEOFFREYWARNERSTUDIO.
   COM

Charles Washburn
890 Collinstown Rd.
Appleton, ME 04862
WWW.CRWASHBURN.COM

Karla Webb
1009 N Main St.
High Point, NC 27262

Mark Wedekind
2136 Alder Dr.
Anchorage, AK 99508
907.279.4308
WWW.BLACKSTONEDESIGN.COM

Walker Weed
30 Three Mile Rd.
Etna, NH 03750

Weersing Furniture Designs
Randy Weersing
1102 River Loop One
Eugene, OR 97404
WWW.WEERSINGFURNITUREDTUDIO.
   COM

Erin Welsh
255 SW California St.
Portland, OR 97219

David Welter
552 S Harold St.
Fort Bragg, CA 95437
707.964.7056

Howard Werner
PO Box 430
Shokan, NY 12481-0430

Mark Werner
PO Box 296
West Branch, IA 52358
319.643.3384

Matthew Werner
260 Dufour St.
Santa Cruz, CA 95060
831.427.3153
WWW.MATTHEWWERNERFURNITURE.
   COM

David Wesseler
PO Box 19
Lorraine, KS 67459-0019

Scott West
Sheridan College
Oakville, ON L6J7T8
Canada

The Westmount Group
Jeff Carter
14 B Gilbert St.
West Haven, CT 06516
WWW.WESTMOUNTGROUP.COM

Larry White
PO Box 1312
Desert Hot Springs,
   CA 92240

Steven White
336 Hammond St.
Bishop, CA 93514
760.872.3828

Susan White
4010 Megan Rd.
Duluth, GA 30096

Walter Whiteley
435 Reynolds Mill Rd.
York, PA 17403

Mark Whitley
1711 Patterson Rd.
Smiths Grove, KY 42171

Stephen Whittlesey
1560 Main St.
W. Barnstable, MA 02668
508.954.3577

Frank Wicks
PO Box 808
1 Sherwood Forest Ln.
Sonoita, AZ 85637
520.405.3522
WWW.WICKSDESIGN.COM

John Wiggers
66 Gartshore Dr.
Whitby, ON L1P 1N6
Canada
905.985.3318

Arthur Willey
PO Box 355
Flat Rock, NC 28731
828.697.8736

Michael Williams
400 N. Enterprise Blvd.
Lebanon, IN 46052

Eric Wilmot
Les Ateliers Du Château
Saint-Amand en
   Puysaie, 58310
France
WWW.ERICWILMOT.FR

Mark Wilson
621 W Fourth St.
Royal Oak, MI 48067

Steven Wilson
Sheridan College
Oakville, ON L6J7T8
Canada

Will Wilson
PO Box 588
Ocean Grove, VIC 3226
Australia

Lothar Windels
24 Stuart Rd.
Newton, MA 02459
617.916.5302
WWW.LOTHARWINDELS.COM

Kimberly Winkle
1862 Puckett Point Rd.
Smithville, TN 37166
615.597.5138

Steve Withycombe
702 S Donovan St.
Seattle, WA 98108

Erik Wolken
127 Ladybug Ln.
Chapel Hill, NC 27516
919.923.5772
WWW.ERIKWOLKEN.COM

Wil Wolski
130 Manion Rd.
Carp, ON K0A1L0
Canada
WWW.WOLSKISTUDIO.COM

Wood Finish Services
Joe Amaral
PO Box 614
Fort Bragg, CA 95437
WWW.WOODFINISHSERVICES.COM

Wood Studio
Randy, Dylan and Keith
   Cochran
402 5th St. SW
Fort Payne, AL 35967
615.347.2097

Donald Wood
520 N Walnut St.
Galena, OH 43021

Paul Wood
15 Broad St. Apt #2904
New York, NY 10005

WSS Design, LLC
Bruce Delaney
573 E 2nd St.
Reno, NV 89502

Zhen Wu,
   see H & J Bronze
   Sculpture Studio

Brian Wurst
33 Woodrow Ave.
Asheville, NC 28801

Stewart Wurtz
3410 Woodland
   Park Ave. N
Seattle, WA 98103
206.283.2586

Sam Wylie
Sheridan College
Oakville, ON L6J7T8
Canada

Yaffe Mays Furniture
258 Shelburne Line Rd.
Colrain, MA 01340

Yuri Yanchyshyn
54 W 21st St. Suite 609
New York, NY 10010

Nancy Yates
PO Box 208271
New Haven, CT 06520
203.432.0615

Nico Yektai
290 Widow Gavits Rd.
PO Box 1088
Sag Harbor, NY 11963
WWW.NICOYEKTAI.COM

Craig Young
PO Box 3044
Fayetteville, AR 72702

Tarik Yousef
8 E. Patterson Ave.
Columbus, OH 43202

Stephen Yusko
835 Jefferson Ave.
Cleveland, OH 44113

Mark Zeh
7 Therese Ave.
Howell, NJ 07731

Hongtao Zhou
455 N Park St.
Art Dept.
6241 Humanities Bldg
Madison, WI 53706

Aviv Zimmerman
Sheridan College
Oakville, ON L6J7T8
Canada

Gregory Znajda
352 Harvey Ave
Des Plaines, IL 60016